Plan B, C, & D
The Men Women Choose When They Don't Have What They *Really* Want!

BY NKANSA LANDIS CASTERLOW

Plan B, C, & D
The Men Women Choose When They Don't Have What They *Really* Want!

Published by PlanBCD.com, LLC.
P.O. Box 162547
Atlanta, GA. 30321

Printed in The United States of America

www.PlanBCD.com

ISBN: 0-9787941-0-9

© 2006—Nkansa Landis Casterlow

Plan B, C, & D
The Men Women Choose When They Don't Have What They *Really* Want!

TABLE OF CONTENTS

Page:

Table of Contents...III
Dedication...1
Acknowledgements...3
Foreword...9
Introduction...11

PART 1: IDENTIFICATION
Chapter 1—The Plans...15
Chapter 2—The Chase...25

PART 2: INFAMOUS CHOICES
Chapter 3—The Problem With Sue...41
Chapter 4—The Curse of Eve...53
Chapter 5—On The Edge...59
Chapter 6—Nightmare On Your Street...65

PART 3: CHANGE MY PLAN? HOW?
Chapter 7—Plan D and C...91
Chapter 8—Becoming Plan B?...101
Chapter 9—The Coveted A...105

PART 4: THE BOTTOM LINE
Chapter 10—The Vibe...115
Chapter 11—Needs and Wants...133
Chapter 12—Sex...155
Chapter 13—Sex Sobriety...177
Chapter 14—Better Choices...217
APPENDIX...229

Dedication

I dedicate this to the single people out there who have a balanced, level head, and who are trying to make good decisions as they look for good things. Stay optimistic! Keep honing in on your own development and purpose, and your needs (and many of your wants) will come. To those who have an ongoing struggle due to past choices, may you be granted peace by our Heavenly Father. Know that it's not too late to experience great things in life. Perhaps your experiences can also be of help to others.

To my father David, whose long time goal to publish has produced through us of your progeny, and will continue to do so.

Acknowledgements

I give thanks to the Most High God Jehovah for all things, and may this content (in whole or in part) prove to be a useful servant to many.

I thank those who I interviewed and shared perspectives with, whose views may have been like mine or extremely different. Thank you to those who related experiences they knew, and to those who shared their own.

Thanks to the ladies I have dated and established a friendship with, for sharing a slice of your life with me. Thanks also to the incompatible women who helped me to realize how challenging it is to find good basics in a woman, which helps me appreciate it more when I do see the basics. You were my inspiration to write this.

Thank you to my sponsors:

Cache' at Stonecrest Mall in Lithonia, Georgia— for providing the lovely dress and bracelet for the cover model.

Evolve Clothiers at Cumberland Mall in Marietta, Georgia—for providing the men's shirts for the cover. You really need to go visit them, or call 770-801-0039 or 404-784-1156. They'll make you (or the man in your life) look sharp.

The Concierge Group—For a wonderful catering experience, visit www.theconciergegrp.com

Special Thanks to:

My photographer—Nukola Herndon. I am so happy with the job she has done! When you want a photographer who'll do a great job and stay committed till the end to produce a great finished product, contact Nukola at 404-551-0677 or nukola1001@yahoo.com

XaneSolutions, LLC—For business and administrative services, visit www.xanesolutions.com or

Acknowledgements

call 404-933-4251.

For financial services, call Mr. T. Michael Haney, CFP at 770-964-9171. He helped to accelerate the process of making this happen for me!

Special Thanks to my friends/support team for logistical assistance:

Kim Griffith, Trina Stuckey, Jodie Thompson, Lorraine Saunders, Bethany Davis, Derek Johnson, and Marlon McDaniel.

My cover models (they did a great job):

Faith McConico (as Sue)—for modeling calls, contact her at 404-428-3767 or fmcconico@hotmail.com

Michael Issa (as Plan B)—for modeling calls, contact him at 678-887-0535 or michael@hishost.net

Andrew Rush (as Plan C)—for modeling calls, contact him at 404-643-6121 or rushhour33@yahoo.com

Kenny Sigler (as Plan D)—for modeling calls or information about Sigler Entertainment, contact him at sigler.kenny@gmail.com

Another model who was not selected, but who has a good model look and a great attitude—Ronald Lowe—for modeling contact him at 404-502-9070 or ronjamlow@aol.com

Chandra R. Thomas from Atlanta Magazine— thanks for your support

The staff at the Sheraton Colony Square in Atlanta

Many thanks also to:

Spirit—for your contribution—not only was it appreciated, but also the encouragement along with your support. (Catch her bi-weekly Sunday nights w/ Joyce Littel on V-103 FM and Friday nights on WAOK 1380 AM in Atlanta).

Acknowledgements

Joyce Littel—you have such a kind spirit, and thank you for coaching & helping the community with relationships for 16 years.

Michael Baisden—for not only being an example as a Black male author discussing relationships, but also for keeping much needed dialog on the table.

Any and all media stations / radio shows, magazines, book clubs or websites that provides an outlet for this book and its promotion.

My mother (Jean) who have always been in my corner—you are such a blessing, and I value so much the lessons I've learned from you.

My daughter Nia—my favorite gift—you have taught me many things, including about myself, and you help me to be a better person.

My brother Daryl, who have always been 'my biggest fan' of my writing—(I see good things coming your way).

My brother Seaton (As-Seema)—thanks for the inspiration to *KEEP ON MOVING!* —(see you in a better way soon by the God of Justice).

My sister Monica—I won't forget our great conversation—thanks for the history and words of blessing.

My brother Mellow Mel and my sister-in-law Rosalind—thank you both for everything—your support, feedback, the works! You're an asset on my team!

My sister Tonya—thank you so much for your great suggestions!

Veronica—continued success is inevitable for you—you have great determination and thank you for helping to keep me on track.

Josh Harper—your help with promotions is very

Acknowledgements

much appreciated.

Thank you to my family and friends who gave me their support and encouragement, even those just asking, "How's your book coming?"

Sonji—thanks for the feedback and support.

Ayinde Ade & Howard Griffin—you guys had me wanting to keep my face covered until I was done! (Thanks for that!)

Noreen B. Ware—thanks for the legal advice!

Rah—(author of "Nommo Rhyme and Reason")

Kenny (of Sigler Entertainment—'Mr. International')

Kobie—thanks for making sure I wasn't slack'n!, Bernita—thanks for the support.

Gail—thanks for your thought provoking feedback and suggestions.

Kim Jenkins, Ms. Beverly, and Bobby—many continued blessings.

Randal Reid, Chris Foster, & Fred Muhammad—you guys helped to keep me afloat—thank you for that and the great feedback!

Khary Menelik (thanks for the input), Clint Eastman (thanks for the input), Brandon Culpepper (thanks for the input), Tim Harrison (thanks for the input), Stanley T., Bro. Malcolm M., George Cromwell II, Ronnie G., Hommer Hammonds—thanks for the feedback, Banky J.—you were one of the first to hear '*The 4 Level Dialog*'—thanks for the confidence you gave me in it!, Brenda M. J., Alex M. (cuz)—thanks for the 4LD feedback!, Rene P., Akiba G., Tiffany B., Carolyn W., Izzy O., Jason B, Joy, Linden J., Marie, Mario, Tiffany S., D.J. Mike B.—thanks for the books, Roy, Bobby G., Janet H., Donna L., Xenia, Cliff, Edie Ammermann, Sophia Aarons,

Acknowledgements

Allan Fine, Sharron, Stephanie F., Janice C., Tim B., Shannon A., and Michelle. Thank you also to anyone who may have been of support after this book was sent to print. If I have overlooked your name, please charge it to my head and not my heart, and know that I am so grateful for you. May Jah bless every one of you. Thank you for any and every encouraging word, and your belief in me. It would have taken longer to get here without you.

Foreword

It gives me great pleasure to write a few words about this book; and I'm sure its pages will become worn with use as it proves itself a valuable resource for you. Achieving true happiness in your relationship is a challenging job – it takes a sense of connectedness between you and your partner, effective communication skills, and a genuine respect for commitment. Whether you are an "amateur" when it comes to love or an experienced veteran, Plan B, C, & D has tools that you will be able to immediately apply to your life, in order to begin achieving the kinds of results you want in your intimate partner relationships. Nkansa utilizes real-life scenarios and a "tell it like it is" style to help you better understand the thought processes of women, why women choose the mates they often choose, and the potential consequences of their decisions. Through the book, he also challenges you to take a critical look at your dating habits and helps you identify the changes that must be made from within in order to attract the kind of love that you truly desire.

As you advance through the contents of this book, pay close attention to the organization of the book and its progression. As it evolves, so too should your confidence in your ability to not only choose the right partner for you, but for you to make healthy choices over the course of your relationship that will both sustain and strengthen your relationship. This book is chock-full of factual information and well researched data related to unhealthy [abusive] relationships, the *real deal* when it comes to the ratio between available men & women and dating, and extremely important information that *every* couple will want to know about in the effort to maximize their intimacy. Plan B, C, & D also chronicles very specific information that every person should know about STDs / STIs (some of my old school folks might be more familiar with the term VDs) BEFORE beginning an intimate relationship with a new partner, or continuing on their sexual relationship with their current partner.

I am confident that when you are finished with this book, you'll be torn between going back to the beginning to read it all over again and letting your best friend read it so that they too can have the opportunity to arm themselves with this valuable information. My suggestion to you would be that you grab two copies of this book— one for you and one for your friend—otherwise, you may never see yours again. I leave you now in excellent hands to begin the journey that will assist you in identifying, obtaining, and maintaining the kind of relationship that you truly want. May you never settle for anything less than the absolute best. You're worth it!

Peace & Blessings,

Spirit

Spirit holds a Master's degree in Professional Counseling and is currently completing her Ph.D. in Counseling Psychology. In addition to providing counseling and life coaching services, Spirit is a freelance journalist and talk show host. For more information, contact Spirit by emailing: talk2spirit@gmail.com.

Plan B, C, & D
The Men Women Choose When They Don't Have What They *Really* Want!

INTRODUCTION

I decided to write this book, not after dating hundreds of women, but after being out of the dating game for over a decade and being once again on the scene for just a short time. I remembered quickly the things I didn't like about dating and how challenging the process can be. Jumping the hurdles of a date's issues, a person who shows their representative instead of their true self, not to mention getting through those who are just incompatible with me, gets old really fast.

Not only was I out of the dating scene for many years, but my environment was different. I grew up in a religious faith where I was to only date those in that faith. No longer being a part of that religion, I was starting to meet women of different backgrounds and thought grooming. While people are people and some basic fibers of women and dating all have commonalities, I was now out of my familiar comfort zone.

Being over a decade older, I had to seek out women who were mature and like me, know what they want in dating and in life. Through my process, I found myself often being placed in women's C Plans, and sometimes Plan D. This was puzzling at first because, while not conceded, I do have a reasonable level of self-confidence and feel I'm a good catch. So what was the problem? I had to understand more about women and the choices they make. I had to hear what they say and read between the lines of what they *really* want. I also talked to guys, some who were considerably older than I, along with women where there was no dating interest,

11

who would tell me the "real deal" about their perspective. From the interviews, discussions and from reading, I gained insight on things that has been helpful for me in my life regarding dating, sex, and some of the issues therein. The whole concept was really simple once I got the big picture, and hopefully by this book, you will get a clearer view of that picture, where you fit in, and why. With that knowledge, we'll discuss how you can alter your place in the plan, and / or make better decisions to create a whole new picture for yourself. Though novels dealing with relationships are a huge market, this is not a fictional novel designed as entertainment. It is non-fiction, and more of a dating handbook discussing certain topics and issues as it relates to singleness. Therefore, the subject matter will vary. Dating is discussed more so than relationships, so I hope it will help you to navigate through the mine field of the initial phase of dating. Still, there is useful information herein that anyone can benefit from, regardless of relationship status or gender.

I strongly encourage you not to skip around in your reading of this book. You will get the most from your reading by reading in succession. This book will discuss a certain type of personality of women. Not all women fit into the description that will be discussed, but this is a general guide and you can use all, some, or bits of this information as needed. Whether you have not thought about some of these things and this book turns the light on for you, or you've believed some of these things and have your thoughts confirmed, as you make any needed adjustments for your situation, I wish you all the best!

Nkansa Landis Casterlow

PART 1:

IDENTIFICATION

Chapter 1:

The PLANS

Chapter 1:
The PLANS

Sue and Plan A:

You can't have a Plan B, C, and D without first having a Plan A. As mentioned in the introduction, some women are not this type of personality and may make a C or D guy *her* Plan A, or first choice. That may be a deeper, maybe even more spiritual woman (as for choosing B, well, that speaks for itself!). As for this type of woman herein, we'll call her "Sue." For the ladies whose real name is Sue, I had to use a name, so I guess you're it! Don't take it personal (unless the shoe fits). The following is her Plan A: First and foremost, he is a man with money, prestige, and / or other resources. Try not to get defensive, my female readers, because if the shoe doesn't fit... (You know). Also understand that whether you're a Sue or not, there is much herein that I'm confident will be useful to you.

While Sue's Plan A is a man with resources, she *could* be a "gold digger", but not necessarily. In my opinion, gold diggers are in the pursuit of getting something (financial or material) from someone. While Sue may actively do this, she may not, but could just choose to keep associates at a certain distance or have lukewarm enthusiasm if they don't meet Plan A requirements. Even if she's not assertively pursuing a

Plan B, C, & D
The Men Women Choose When They Don't Have What They *Really* Want!

Plan A, if she stumbles across him she responds to him quite differently from the way she responds to the other Plans, and she can transform like a chameleon to adapt to A's needs and temperament.

Plan A may not have the qualities or physical appearance that she is looking for, but he keeps her at his disposal and she is quick to be available to his call. If you're Plan B, C, or D, and you've had Sue to cancel a date with you suddenly and give an excuse you doubt, she could have gotten a call from A. Even if A is not a good lover, he gets the primary slot in Sue's time and attention, as false as that attention may be. He could be married or in a serious relationship, but may be the biggest "player" of all. Because of his means, he has access to the women the other plans can and cannot get close to.

Of course, Sue would *love* her Plan A to have it all; money, looks, great lover, tough guy, nice build, romantic, and intelligent all in one. But how often is that found? Even *she* knows that. The reality is, if he has financial strength and stability and none of the rest, he still makes Sue's Plan A list. That goes for a relationship partner and for the part time slot as well.

When she doesn't have Plan A available, she may or may not try to get financial or material gains from Plan C or D, but generally her next preference of the guys she spends time with is Plan B. (Actually, at times Sue may have Plan A, and still have a Plan B on the side!)

Chapter 1: The PLANS

Plan B:

Plan B is "the maintenance man". He's the one she usually prefers or defaults to as a lover. He's not as inclined to spend money on her as Plans A, C or D may be, and frankly he doesn't have to. He knows he has something she wants and he doesn't need money to keep her coming back. He sometimes (but not always) has a thug or bad boy image that she likes, or maybe he's the strong, silent type. He does not or cannot give her any commitment as her man, but she calls him when she needs a "fix". If she's not in the mood to date someone new, she calls on him so she'll know what to expect. He may be married, in a serious relationship with someone, or just not inclined to commitment.

Sue acts out her fantasies with B. She'll respond favorably to graphic sexual talk and suggestions by him that C & D wouldn't expect her to accept. (Plan A may talk to her that way based on his confidence or presumptuousness.) She'll release the extremities of her freaky sexuality with B, doing things she normally may not do with the other Plans, maybe not even with Plan A. Since she thinks of B as a manly thug, bad boy, or sexual maintenance man, her thoughts of him may not be romantic but may be strictly sexual; this is what allows her to explore her wild side most freely with him. Since he may only see her in a sexual way also, she feels sexy with him because that is his interest in her. The thought of him becomes synonymous with sex or fantasy. She doesn't think of issues, drama, or personality concerns with him, it's just a detachment from the real world, and for that moment she entertains her fantasies and focuses on having good sex. He could be a good lover but even if

Plan B, C, & D
The Men Women Choose When They Don't Have What They *Really* Want!

he's not the greatest, her state of mind with him heightens her experience. This may be her most cherished vice.

Unless she later has a serious change in her life that she is deeply committed to, B may long keep a place in her spirit, even being able to loose touch and call again years later to make another 'booty call.'

Though she'll prioritize seeing Plan B over C and D, Sue doesn't spend a lot of time with B, unless they take a trip somewhere. It's normally just the time it takes for a service call, the "lube job" and "rotation" sort of thing. When she's not spending time with a Plan A and she's not getting maintenance from Plan B, she spends her dating time with Plan C.

Plan C:

C is the guy who probably has the most appeal to Sue for a relationship (aside from A of course). He's got some appealing qualities and he may have a little of all the Plan characteristics. He is someone she may like to be seen or associated with, especially with her family or friends. He is a likable person, and has some good things going for himself. Still, his lack of expendable resources or prestige doesn't satisfy the flash Sue is looking for.

If she doesn't have Plan A, and isn't spending time with B or C, then in her time of boredom or when she has something she wants to vent about, she calls Plan D.

Chapter 1: The PLANS

Plan D:

D is the last choice. Just as on a report card 'F' is a failing grade, so someone less than D doesn't even make her list. We won't spend time on Plan F, because he's someone Sue won't give much consideration to. He has little or nothing to offer Sue.

D is "the nice guy". They say "nice guys finish last" and in Sue's case, this is the truth. D is the guy she'd like to keep in her bag and pull out when she's completely bored and has no other things she'd rather do. She dumps her worries on him, and he's a good listener and good with advice like a male girlfriend, only with the male perspective. He's always there for her and (sometimes) glad to get her call even when it's because her other Plans weren't available or stood her up. She may never have even tried him sexually, and maybe she could be very pleased if she did, but she views him to be boring and a wasted weekend night. D may be mentally deep and mature, but he is far from what she looks for in a man and she would probably not be faithful to him.

It could be that Sue made an opportunity for D to have sex with her and it may not have gone successfully. Maybe they lacked chemistry, or perhaps he wanted to get into her as a person and all she wanted was sex. She could have given hints that she wanted sex and he didn't get the hint, didn't know how to act on it, or just didn't act for some reason. This could have caused her to view him as Plan D. This is sometimes due to a communication barrier. Some men are not good with words, yet many women feel men should automatically be outspoken or aggressive based on our gender. It's not always so. That's why women may want to be comfortable with broaching deeper subjects also, not exclusively waiting on the man to start it. She can simply ask his views on sex do's and don'ts, or sex and dating, or even simply what he likes in a woman. However you feel comfortable getting a discussion going. Since dating involves attraction (generally), sex is a subject that sooner or later will come up, so have a thought in mind of how to approach it or receive it in a graceful manner. This can open doors to guys that the woman may never have encountered otherwise, because some men may want to approach or get deep but may not know how, or may just not realize how fast she wants to go.

The Plans Commentary

In most cases, Plan categories will have specific qualities. Yet there are always people who can blend into more than one category, or in some ways seem to contradict the Plan you may expect them to be in. For example, which of the Plans would be more likely to be a dead-beat dad? Actually, any of them could be. There are some very well to do people (Plan A) who do back flips to avoid actually parenting their child or paying for their support as they should. Celebrities included. And even though Plan C has some appealing qualities and a likable character, sometimes people surprise you when you see what they're capable of, when it comes to them being in an unfavorable situation.

What about the way Sue views Plan B? Does it have to be with a man who is detached and only into her for sex, that she can feel this sexual and uninhibited? How practical is it to expect a woman to be able to experience these higher levels of intimacy and fantasy

Chapter 1: The PLANS

with a committed partner she sees every day? In some cases a woman may be involved in a sexual relationship because that's just what it turned into. It's basically physical mechanics; the extinguisher to the fire. But I believe some women create Plan B in their minds first, to fulfill a need. Not just a physical need, but also a psychological one. Especially if she lacks fulfillment in other areas of her life, Plan B becomes her escape, her knight in shining armor.

Plan B, C, & D
The Men Women Choose When They Don't Have What They *Really* Want!

CATEGORY QUICK REFERENCE

Category	Description
Sue	A woman who puts a man's financial means, material posses-sions, or other resources first in her choice of a partner or relationship. Others, even a man of good character, who has average resources or less takes a back seat. (Plan B, C, or D)
Plan A the jackpot	This is a man with above average financial, material, or other resources. This is Sue's first choice in a companion or partner.
Plan B fireman	The maintenance man. Sue's default choice in a lover. He typically won't commit. He sometimes has a bad boy or thug image, but not always.
Plan C almost	Likable person by friends and family. May have some of all the Plan characteristics. Due to lack of affluence, he's not quite who Sue wants to settle down with.
Plan D last resort	The nice guy. Sue's last choice. He is a good confidant, and she vents with him because he's a good listener and gives good advice. Mature and dependable, yet Sue feels he's boring and a wasted weekend.

Chapter 2:

The Chase

Chapter 2:
The Chase

We'll talk more about Sue and the Plans she chooses later, but first let's talk about the part of dating I call the chase. The chase is a phase that has some of the most preventable problems in dating. So many times, our woes begin by simply chasing the wrong type of person, or someone who obviously doesn't want to be caught; or else it wouldn't be much of a chase. I think of the humorous scene in the film *My Best Friend's Wedding* with Julia Roberts, where she was chasing the groom to be, and he was chasing the bride to be. That is such a reality in life. So often, we try to win the attention or affection of someone who may lack appreciation for it or who may be trying to do the same for someone else.

Even if you feel you have no options, there's probably someone who, if you think about it, has shown or expressed interest in you not so long ago. You may have dismissed it because they weren't what you wanted or what you visualized in your mind, or maybe you just weren't ready for a relationship. Therefore, if you just stopped short in your chase of someone who's running from you, then figuratively an option would run right into you. Not that you should be with someone you don't want just because *they* want *you*, I would never recommend that! Far to the contrary, you *must only* involve yourself with someone who you also want to be with.

Knowing the difference between your wants and needs is essential. Once you know that, you can be better equipped to handle a crucial part of dating, which is the *selection process.* That process can be explained in one simple sentence: **KNOW WHAT TO LOOK FOR, AND IF IT'S ALREADY CHASING YOU!**

Greedy Eyes

Greed can make a person feel like a child in a candy store, when he or she couldn't consume a fraction of the candy there (though many do strive to have it all). You may see many attractive people, but when you break down their personalities and the baggage many have along with their wayward thinking, how many in the sea of people are really good for / compatible with you? Let's say you're at an event where there's a crowd of attractive single people. You may let your eyes soak up all they can hold. You may not even talk to someone interested in you because they aren't among the best looking people there. Maybe guys saw a better body and / or prettier face, and the same with ladies or they saw a guy who looks financially successful (ching-ching). Perhaps you didn't talk to the ones you wanted to for some reason, or you did but they were looking for the "better thing" also. Now as you leave disappointed, the person who was interested in you didn't look so bad after all, did they? Again, if it's not what you want, then why bother? At the same time, many very good prospects are overlooked or not viewed as the eligible single person they are, and this is an unfortunate part of the dating

Chapter 2: The Chase

scene. Why does this happen? Because many people make decisions based on 90% appearance and 10% "other", because of their priorities. When they see an issue (which should be a legitimate yellow or red flag), it's hard to turn away from it sometimes if the attraction factor is strong enough. They find themselves compromising some pretty significant things at times. We're all human; many of us have done this at some point.

Watch out for those with greedy eyes, who want you as an option on their buffet. Some will say or do all that's necessary to have their way with you. This applies to men and women alike. If you're dealing with a "player", they may have a number of sexual partners presently, or they may just pursue one conquest at a time. Be sure to listen with more than just the fuzzy feelings you may receive, but with a reasoning mind. If you can't connect the dots and something's missing or not making sense, you better ask what it is and why. If you only have a cell or work number and are never invited to call or visit their home, they may be married or have a live-in S.O. These days, you should give a cell number until you feel comfortable giving your home number, but if it's been some time and they never offer their number, give it some thought. Stay aware, yet no matter how careful you try to be, there are many who will misrepresent themselves and violate your space. When they reveal themselves, be quick to expel them from your life. As wrong as their deceit is, it's also wrong for people to allow themselves to become victims because of not using what is sometimes basic common sense. Everyone has the responsibility of guarding their well-being.

Plan B, C, & D
The Men Women Choose When They Don't Have What They *Really* Want!

What Do You Bring To The Table?

In the infamous *Chase,* we typically receive a likeness of the energy we send out. While I'm not a scholar of metaphysics, I do believe that when you're concentrating on money and material things, you will encounter people that have and pretend to have the means that you're focused on. Keep in mind, however, that you also often get treated like someone who is focused on materialism, and those with money and power usually know the thought process of these people and act accordingly. For the woman seeking a man with financial stability, you should bring to the table an asset that shows you're working in harmony with the lifestyle you want to live (besides spending ability). Are you progressing in your own financial goals (independent of him)? Are you an asset to his business or line of work? How about this for a subject many women don't seem to want to hear these days: Can you cook? And if you live together in a relationship / marriage (if it gets that far) are you willing to cook consistently? You may find a man who likes to cook or doesn't mind it, but if you make that a requirement, your options could drop dramatically. If all you have to offer is a good climax, then you're quite expendable. He can even get that from a graphic dream. Develop other attributes to offer.

The same applies to a man. He may have many requirements for his partner, but he also needs to make himself an asset to the arrangement. This can be done in more than financial ways. Simply put: Bring value to her life.

In the chase process, BE HONEST. This is hardly done in a total way. While it's understandable that

Chapter 2: The Chase

you want to give a good impression, why create drama by someone later learning that you are not the person they first met? Why give someone the power of making you hide in fear that they'll learn the truth about who you really are? If they don't want you, the real you, then find someone who does! This is elementary, but some would rather enjoy a stolen, tricked moment than to stay true to themselves and others.

Is An Opposite Age Right For You?

They say opposites attract, but the common ground you share will keep you together. In some cases the more common ground you share, the better. But that's based on the person's personality. In other cases too many similarities can be problematic, for example, if both people are stubborn. Regarding opposites, sometimes age opposites attract, the older with the younger. Older men have been dating younger women forever, but older women are dating younger men more now, also. They (the older women) are taking good care of themselves and defying their age by their appearance. They're confident and often don't have time for games, they just like to know in clear terms what the status is with their companion. I think mature women can be very sexy. There are considerations in dating regarding age, however, that should be determined. For example, if you are considering this person as a relationship or marriage partner, discuss your views on children. If he wants children (biologically his), and she doesn't or isn't able due to her age, then consider your needs in this area in the selection process. With the younger person, be sure they're not too young to understand the depth of real commitment, if you're seeking commitment or a marriage mate. Even when a young person wants to be in a deep relationship, sometimes they later find they didn't have time to enjoy or explore life as much as they would've liked. In my opinion, I think a good age for a man to get married is 30 or older, and for a woman, as close to that as possible. By then, you have established much of the personality you'll have for the rest of your life, you've "learned to walk" from other relationships, gotten your career or business under way, and have a better grip on finances / credit, housing, etc. Your priorities are different from when you were 20-25, and now you have a better head start.

What's At Stake?

The cost of selecting the wrong companion can be not only unhealthy physically but also psychologically. It can lead to a stressful relationship that you wouldn't anticipate. Poor choices can lead to broken homes, families and communities. That, in turn, fuels the cycle of many other problems in society such as drugs, crime, lifestyles that produce diseases, etc. Not to say that it is all due to the initial selection of the partner. At times issues happen, and that's a part of life. There are times, however, when issues can be avoided or reduced by making the best decision about who you fuse into your life. Ask good questions and observe the answer, body language, and the spirit behind the answer. We can't read minds and hearts, but you can use discernment to get the feel of things. Watch out for the yellow (caution) flags and the red (STOP—and get the hell out of there) flags. When you get that inner voice guiding you that

Chapter 2: The Chase

things aren't right, don't push the mute button, but listen and act on it. Ask for their views and why they are what they are. Sift well, and if you know it definitely doesn't fit, why waste your time?

Logistics

There have been many successes in people coming together by someone playing matchmaker. Generally, if the matchmaker knows both people, they can have a pretty good idea of what each person wants and it could accelerate the dating process.

Regarding places single people can meet, I think the best places are events where you share interests; such as a religious establishment, community or social events, or the gym. Also, keep your eyes open even at the department store, grocery store, or post office. In such an informal setting, usually both people are not dressed in their jazziest attire with the pretentious mental wall up as you'd find in most night clubs. You may even catch the ladies with their hair undone, no makeup, and like an unrehearsed morning; a true depiction of themselves!

Problem Solved!

Have you ever met two, three, or more people who were together (maybe friends, family, or co-workers) and you found more than one of them attractive? Of course you have! When this happens, what do we do, and what *should* we do if we're interested in getting to know one of them? Usually, we either focus on the one that we're attracted to the most and show them more attention, or we find ourselves accepting the attention of the one that gives us the interest signals. In both cases, I think it needs to be handled differently! Let's say the one you're most attracted to is already involved, or doesn't have the same interest in you. Then, once you've shown attention to your first choice, usually you've messed up your chances for her / his associates. Even if she / he is interested, perhaps you'd later find that you're not compatible. The same is true for the one who first shows interest in you. Even if they're attractive enough, they may not be the one best suited for you. The way I think it should be handled is to talk to them all as a group. Ask them questions allowing them all to answer, and make no attention distinctions at this point! If you don't have long to talk and have to part ways, ask if you can all get together at a future time as a group, which will allow you to get to know them all and then you can learn which one, if any, would be more compatible with you. This can lead you to the best possible vibe amongst the people you've just met. Don't be afraid to exchange contact information with all of them, because if you only get contact information from one of them, then you give the impression of showing a partial interest. If only one of them gets your info, then they can block you from the others or the others from you. By exchanging information with all of them, you can talk to them individually if you choose, but be careful. The first one you talk to, especially for a long time or late at night, may pass on the word. If your objective is to get to know the others, be mindful of your conversation. Problem solved!

Chapter 2: The Chase

I have heard so many times that pretty women don't get the attention you may expect that they would. This is due to men being intimidated usually, or assuming the woman already has someone or wouldn't want to talk to them. In reality, pretty women can even be lonely due to such erroneous thinking. Go for it. You'll never know until you try.

Imagine No More?

Speaking of going for it, I had an interesting experience where I was guilty of the thinking mentioned above. I was preparing for a meeting, and my partner fell out of touch and unavailable for me to reach shortly before the meeting would have started. Not knowing if we would have the meeting, I drove across town in heavy traffic near the usual meeting point and awaited a call back. To kill time, I went to a store. Inside, I saw a lady from a distance that looked absolutely stunning from a side view. I only saw a part of her face, and I passed by with amazement. Wanting to know who she is but *knowing* she has got to either have someone or be condescending, I rationalized—as many men do—that I should just keep walking, remain in awe, and let her walk out the door. I realized though, that that's self-defeating thinking, and I'm more conscious than that! I _had_ to go back and say something to her. While my lower conscious mind resisted in fear of rejection, another part of me *ordered* me to go back. I did.

As I waited for her to complete her transaction, admiring her closer confirmed why I had to speak to her. She appeared to be a ten (on a scale of one to ten). Still, her face was not completely visible. As she turned around to face me, her face was like a 12! WOW! And her body still held high on the meter. I introduced myself, we talked for a couple minutes, and she was really nice. Still, feeling like I jumped a hurdle just by approaching her, I didn't even give her my contact info or ask for hers. I know, I know, I was asleep at the wheel!

To condense the story, she did tell me about her business, and I later contacted her that way. We went out once, and though it didn't develop into a relationship in this case, as I said above, go for it. You never know. Just maybe if you're ready, you could find what you've hoped for and you can *imagine no more!*

Remember, there can be a thin line between someone determined to get their girl (or guy) and someone who is too pushy or tactlessly forceful. That can be a sign of someone who is psychologically unstable, and the next step could be stalking! Don't overstep the other person's comfort zone. Also, don't say what you don't mean. If you do, then what you meant to get across could backfire. Keep it simple and genuine.

Chapter 2: The Chase

<u>Freeze</u>

THERE IS THIS THING ABOUT ME THAT I REALLY WANT TO
CHANGE;
WHILE I'M COOL WITH SELF-ESTEEM, MY CONFIDENCE IS
STRANGE
SOMETIMES IT SEEMS IT'S HEALTHY AND IT'S ABLE TO
ENDURE;
BUT WHEN IT COMES TO MEETING LADIES, I'M NOT
ALWAYS SURE
I CAN SPEAK AND SMILE, AND SOMETIMES I SPEAK MY
MIND;
BUT HALF THE TIME I WANT TO TALK, AND WORDS I
CANNOT FIND
FOR ME TO HIDE THE WAY I FEEL, CAN BE BAD FOR MY
HEALTH;
TO ACT LIKE I DON'T CARE, LIES TO HER, AND TO MYSELF
I HATE IT CAUSE I KNOW LIKE THIS, I REALLY CAN MISS
OUT;
ON MAYBE EVEN A SOUL-MATE, BECAUSE OF FEAR AND
DOUBT
LIFE COULD BE BETTER, BUT LONELINESS I ACCEPT;
WHEN I FREEZE, I FEEL THE PUNCH, AND TAUNTING OF
REGRET
THOUGH I FEEL I HAVE A GIFT, CREATIVE IN EXPRESSION;
THE DREADFUL FREEZE CAN HAVE A HOLD, AND LOCK
ME IN DEPRESSION
I PRAY THAT I MAY MASTER THIS, AND PUT MY SOUL AT
EASE;
AND COME TO SEE WHAT IT COULD BE, WHEN ONCE I
END THE FREEZE.

NLC

PART 2:

INFAMOUS CHOICES

Chapter 3:

The Problem With Sue

Chapter 3:
The Problem With Sue

Sue's Reasoning

Sue has a number of issues. She may, like most women, speak of wanting a good man, yet doesn't recognize or appreciate him if she encounters him. This is because in her view, the only truly good man for her is someone with resources, who's willing to throw them her way.

There are men out there that don't treat women with dignity, are overly possessive, abusive, unloving to children, and more. That doesn't even go into the men that are bisexual (down low), addicted to drugs or alcohol or have some other serious issue. What about their health status? Yet, when a good man that doesn't have these issues talks to Sue, she can easily discount him for downright foolish and trivial reasons. She may say; "He didn't pursue (chase) me hard enough" or he may be discounted because there was some type of trivial misunderstanding which caused her to stop communicating with him. Of course, if it was a Plan A involved, this wouldn't be a problem.

We've all heard and / or read, "You reap what you

sow". Sowing can be done by your thoughts, words and actions. If sowing is done properly, it can help you to achieve your goals. Yet we must be careful of what we ask for and understand what's connected with our reaping, or end result. Even if you receive what you hope for financially, that's what could be the dominant feature or benefit from that "tree". You may have found a man with money, but how will he treat you? Will he respect and love or care about you and any children that may be involved? Each "seed" produces according to its kind. If you want to have a field that produces better "fruit trees", you must sow by your thoughts, actions and pursuits being focused on better priorities, with you yourself being ready for those things to come to you. Keep in mind, it will delay and limit your results to have unrealistic priorities.

My male readers: Try not to allow yourself to be frustrated when talking to Sue or thinking about how narrow her thinking is. Remember that it is her that will experience the consequences of her pursuits, so let her live her life.

I had an interesting conversation with a young lady I went out with, who broke down Sue's thinking. Surprising to me, she was not what I expected in the stereotype of Sue. She was someone I thought was mature, had a measure of success, and appeared to be quite self-sufficient. She said, *"Women give men what they want: sex. When they do, they are giving of themselves emotionally and often not receiving the emotional connection that they really want. This leaves them feeling open and somewhat used, and they should therefore receive financial benefits from the man as a*

Chapter 3: The Problem With Sue

replacement for what he's not giving her—commitment, a relationship, security, etc."

      This is the "helpless victim" cry; as if the woman has no choice in what she "gives". We're not talking about rape here. This is the biggest pile of waste voided from a bull I've ever heard! First of all, many of these women don't even *want* commitment. They do what they do because they want money or some type of resources, that's it. If they do want commitment, it's to lock down the benefits. Remember, we're describing Sue here. She has a choice whether or not she has sex with him. What other women want money in exchange for sex? He owes her *nothing* for sex, unless of course she's a prostitute; and then she should just tell him her fee up front. Lastly, she should be getting something from the sex also, so it shouldn't be just for him. If she's not getting gratified from it (non-monetarily), then why do it? For the money? They should both do it because they want to; but check your motives.

Another Kind of Sue?

      Sue is not necessarily a broke woman looking for a free or plush ride. There is another type of Sue, which I call Sue-2. The only difference with Sue-2, is that she is financially established herself, with above average finances. So if she has her own resources, why call her a Sue? What's wrong with her wanting a man who's well-to-do? This does get tricky, but here it is: Even if she isn't seeking his A status to provide something she doesn't yet have, *if she doesn't take the time to determine his character and judges him solely on finances and / or lack of an affluent lifestyle,* she's a Sue to me. Don't misunderstand me. I'm not implying that a woman should accept a man who has nothing going for himself. But where does she draw the line, and what is the first phase of her screening process? Some women want to see or know what a man drives, and some even judge by the shoes he's wearing, with no knowledge of what he may have at home. If his attire or material things don't impress her on the spot, mentally her door is closed.

For women who are famous and wealthy, they may seek someone on their level just as wealthy men may do, because many people are after their money. That's understandable for them to make that decision, though some argue if it's necessary. We all know things people can do to get close to celebrities and get a slice of their pie. **PLEASE HEAR ME OUT.** I'm not saying that non-celebrities or people who are not wealthy are wrong for making that decision for themselves when they have a lifestyle that people may want to cunningly move into. Typically a successful achiever wants a person who will complement them; But to what extent? It all comes down to priorities. If there's a guy who drives a $15,000 car and you (ladies) drive a $60,000 car, is he not a consideration to you? If not, why; when he could have the qualities you say are very important to you?

While admittedly there are some men who couldn't handle a woman making more money than he, not all men are that way. There are a large number of women doing financially well these days, and sometimes her having a higher income than him isn't just a problem due to *his* ego. I was present during a conversation with a professional woman one day, and she talked to her assistant about a date she had with her live-in boyfriend.

46

Chapter 3: The Problem With Sue

She spoke of them having an argument on their way out to a gathering, and he wanted to go back home due to the mood it put them in. She told him she wasn't turning around, and 'it was her car so she was doing things her way.' Her conversation made it clear that she was the larger bread-winner. Ego or no ego on his part, that condescending attitude makes her unbearable. She obviously had no respect for her man. Again, we have to check ourselves for the real reasons we make the choices that we do, and keep a realistic view to understand how we create or allow issues into our life.

There are many Sue-2's out there, most who may not even realize they are such. She may be in a relationship already as the woman mentioned above, and she places a value on her relationship based on his finances. She won't put the same effort into her relationship with someone with average or less than average finances as she would someone with more. Think about that. If he is what he should be as far as the way he treats her, why should lack of affluence affect her putting her all into the relationship? I heard a woman on the radio say that because she makes more money than her live in man (I believe her husband), she does not do as much cooking or house work. This is an arrogance that creates division in our relationships and community, especially in the Black community. Women have strived to lift themselves up and have done a good job of doing so, but I believe many have overshot in aiming for success. They have taken charge of their lives, taken charge of the workplace often in management and executive roles, and often the significance of men have depreciated in their view, unless he has a certain financial or material status. I understand to the extent

Plan B, C, & D
The Men Women Choose When They Don't Have What They *Really* Want!

that women have learned to be self sufficient financially so she may not *need* a second income in her home, unlike many years ago. Yet a good man should not be so indivisibly tied to resources. If you have someone who is industrious, with a good plan, money can come. Especially if the woman is as good as she claims to be, and she supports and assists him in a prosperous plan.

Some women even go so far as to say that if she makes more money than her live-in S.O. (significant other), that not only should she do less or no domestic work, but she should also have more of a headship role in the relationship. In one debate that I had I was told, "The one with the money has the power." That "one" may legally have power over material possessions, but what *should* that have to do with the relationship arrangement; and who could be authorized to establish that standard? Just because the corporate world may put more or higher digits on one person's check, does that constitute the authority to determine the arrangements in your home? Even if the woman can buy anything they lay eyes on, if she uses her means to establish herself as the head of the arrangement (whether it's directly verbalized or not) then in my opinion it won't be very successful. This is, of course, based on the type of man she has. Some men don't mind taking a submissive role if he has what he wants materially. Yet, for a man that has self respect, in my opinion he will still need to have a leadership role regardless of who makes more money and even if he is employed by her.

While concern for his preparedness to handle responsibilities, including financial, is proper, Sue exemplifies someone who has money / status as a main priority, above the character of a man. Though it may

Chapter 3: The Problem With Sue

sound like it, this is not meant to be a diatribe towards women who want a progressive life. As we know, there are some worthless men who have taken advantage of good and generous women. Ladies: ***DON'T RAISE A CHILD FOR A SIGNIFICANT OTHER!!!*** This is like a male version of Sue, but much worse. In my opinion, since the man is supposed to carry the brunt of the load as a provider (or at least do his best), a lazy man who seeks to freeload off of a woman disgraces himself. The point I'm making is I'm an advocate of the hard working guy with substance, who gets passed up because he doesn't fit the financial "bill". If a successful woman wants someone who is also successful, then I do understand. You want to be "evenly yoked". Much success and happiness to you. Yet for the Sues out there, especially those with a condescending attitude, just maybe when you get through the rest of this book, it'll have a bearing on your thinking. Maybe you'll find a guy with character who already has his finances going well, but maybe you'll find one with his financial game plan still under construction. Then what will you do? Some women will take care of a man as if he was her child, and others will pass up a good hard working guy because he doesn't have a Superman ® "S" on his chest (and in his bank account). I'm just saying; can we have some balance?

Where Did It Come From?

Many women have been groomed to lock their tracking devices on Plan A by their parents (usually the mother). They want their daughter to have a good life, so they stress to them the need to have a well-to-do man, to be able to pass on a better life to their children. It reminds me of the movie *The Feast of All Saints*, based on the book by Ann Rice and Tyler Perry's movie, *Madea's Family Reunion*. While mothers generally mean well, there is an over emphasis on material status that creates imbalance in some cases. Some women climb rocky mountains to find a Plan A; then, if and when they get him, they're often only pacifying their emotional needs. The Sue mentality influence also comes from friends or other family in many cases, or maybe a woman had bad experiences (baggage) and decided to make her next lover the dollar bill.

I've heard interviews with male celebrities who spoke of being overlooked when they were broke and / or unknown. They didn't get consideration despite them being ambitious and goal oriented. Many women never took the time to learn of their ambition and potential. It's critical to evaluate our value system; our grooming. That's the problem with Sue.

Chapter 3: The Problem With Sue

CATEGORY QUICK REFERENCE

Category	Description
Sue	A woman who puts a man's financial means, material posses-sions, or other resources first in her choice of a partner or relationship. Others, even a man of good character, who has average resources or less takes a back seat. (Plan B, C, or D)
Sue-2	The same as Sue, yet the only distinguishing factor is that Sue-2 has above average resources of her own. She is still consid-ered a Sue based on her priorities.
Plan A the jackpot	This is a man with above average financial, material, or other resources. This is Sue's first choice in a companion or partner.
Plan B fireman	The maintenance man. Sue's default choice in a lover, and he typically won't commit. He sometimes has a bad boy or 'thug' image, but not always.
Plan C almost!	Likable person by friends and family. May have some of all Plan characteristics. Due to lack of affluence, he's not quite what Sue wants to settle down with.
Plan D last resort	The nice guy. Sue's last choice. He is a good confidant, and she vents with him, because he's a good listener and gives good advice. Mature and dependable, yet Sue feels he's a wasted weekend.

Chapter 4:

The Curse of Eve

Chapter 4:
The Curse of Eve

To the woman He said: "...Your craving will be for your husband, and he will dominate you." (Gen. 3:16) In the curse against Eve in this scripture, she was to have a craving; an intense desire. Perhaps in an unnatural way, yet he would dominate her. The two are psychologically connected.

Still Under The Curse?

What's interesting is, some women can keep a guy who has serious issues such as verbal, mental, or physical abuse and it would be hard for him to do enough to make her leave. It's as if when she knows he has a major issue, it allows her to show that she can 'rise up' to the occasion and support her man. (This does not necessarily refer to those in their situation due to fear. That will be discussed later.) Her accepting abuse also involves psychological issues where low self esteem is a factor. Yet, a good guy could do a trivial thing and she's ready to disconnect their ties. It somehow gives her a feeling of being better than him or having power, because she "didn't have to put up with that", or because she cut him off before he cut her off. If she could rise to the occasion and deal with major things with some guys and settle in the things she claims she wants, why can't she have the strength to deal with the simple things from a good man and have *more* of what she wants? Many people are poor communicators, and this can be an example of that. She often doesn't express the extent of how she feels about the small issue, and rather than trying to improve things by communication, she cuts it off. But it goes even deeper than that. They want to be the one looked up to, or needed. This is why sometimes a beautiful woman will be with a man where you ask yourself, "How did *he* get *her*?" You see, she knows he's glad to have her and she'll always feel like the elevated one. The guy who brings the drama that she tolerates knows this, so while he may be bad for her in some ways, he feeds her psychologically by making her feel needed. Again, self esteem is usually a factor in a drama filled relationship, but I would say it's also in a woman's nature to want to feel needed and exalted. Remember this, men, because no matter how you or she looks, women want to feel elevated (not necessarily above you in a one sided way, but highly regarded); like the song "Ascension" by Maxwell. Also, the woman's unlikely match may have been one of the only people to have had the nerve to approach her. (As discussed in "The Chase".)

Women are looking for something consistent to count on. If she has that stable someone, sometimes she will accept extremes so as to keep the consistency and to feel accepted. Think of Eve's feelings in the garden. She persuaded Adam to do what he knew was wrong. She heard Adam point blame on her in his excuse for doing it, and then came the curse on her and her husband. Imagine her feeling of guilt, regret, and shame. Though Adam still likely had love for her, likely he kept some resentment towards her despite him being ultimately accountable for what happened. She probably felt a lot of

Chapter 4: The Curse of Eve

emotional pushback, and along with her craving for him from the curse, eagerly sought Adam's validation and forgiveness. No doubt they had plenty of multi-emotion, high octane sex! It was also the introduction to drama filled relationships.

Make Yourself A Complement

People generally look not only for companionship, but for what they have long lacked in various areas of their life. That's one reason a person should consider all parts of the other person's life if they're interested in a relationship. Consider what you could do to complement your partner's life in various ways, and if their needs are something that you could fill or assist with. Don't just think of what you can get from it, but what can you offer? Don't just think about the typical role of a significant other, to go out, to have sex, or to do typical things. See if you can add something to them that contributes to their life. Can you help them break a bad habit like smoking or over-drinking (even if they're not quite an alcoholic)? Can you teach them something new? Can you help them overcome a stumbling block or be the encouragement to take a big, much needed step like a business venture? These are things that can strengthen ties. Don't misunderstand me though; I'm not encouraging anyone to raise an irresponsible childlike person in order to date them. They need to have some basics and be mature and ready for the challenges and responsibilities of dating. The point is, don't just walk in with your palms out and empty to receive, but have one palm full of things to give and contribute. Then, you'll be handling it like a partnership.

Chapter 5:

On The Edge

Chapter 5:
On The Edge

Just to give my disclaimer: I am not a certified counselor, and have not received any formal training in domestic issues. My knowledge of domestic abuse comes from experiences (mostly of other people) and is merely my opinion based on what I believe to be reasonable judgment.

See It For What It Is—Then Act!

So many times in the dating process, you find things about a person that doesn't pan out, and sometimes you consciously or subconsciously know you should cut ties immediately. Maybe something just doesn't feel right, or genuine. I'm not saying you should run if the wind blows, but if you practice being aware and even prayerful, then I believe you know when to follow your vibe.

Maybe it's something more obvious, like you see they're seriously irresponsible, don't want to work, not respectful to their parents, or have some bad temper, abusive, or obsessive tendencies. If you see these things, ***RUN LIKE A TEN FOOT PIT BULL IS CHASING YOU!!!*** I joke NOT when it comes to serious things like this. You can have an unsuccessful relationship without serious warning signs like these, so why would you jump into something when you see the writing on the wall?

I'm going to take a minute to speak on a sensitive subject to me, and that's domestic abuse. I've talked to so many ladies, even very young ladies, who have experienced domestic violence; violence from the same guy who once charmed them, smiled at them, and even kissed them and sometimes said "I love you." The female often says "He changed." Did someone talk him into thinking it was a good idea to beat his lover? Did he suddenly read a book or see a film that made a good man go bad? Absolutely not.

Even a typically non violent man can be provoked to *some* degree in an instantaneous situation. That's not what I'm referring to here. For someone who snaps for little or no reason, or even with cause for frustration he can't stop the unleashing of his temper, he likely had these tendencies all along. I call it being "on the edge". Often the woman doesn't want to admit that she was not discerning enough to see it sooner. Or maybe she did see it, but felt that either she could change or "save" him, or she was too afraid to be without someone. Sometimes people date psychologically unstable people because that person's attention is flattering and / or boosts their ego or self-confidence. They like the way the attention makes them feel, but they don't realize how unhealthy the extent of the unstable person's adoration is. If someone is clinging to you like the squirrel to the acorn in the animated film *Ice Age*, **you have a problem!** If they act like they're dependent on you to live, be very careful. Sometimes women recognize abusive tendencies after the relationship has taken root but are too afraid to break up with him, having already bought into the fear that he

Chapter 5: On The Edge

would hurt her or someone close to her. The point here is: In the chase process, PLEASE REMEMBER that you *must* be firm about *quickly* cutting off someone that has abusive tendencies. Like in the case of a relative of mine and so many others I know and know of, it can lead to battery, broken bones, and *death* if you don't.

It Could Be Anyone

I used to think, *"Men who beat women are cowards and would not fight another 'real' man. They will only try to show their strength to a woman to dominate her, but would get beat down if they fought a real man."* These were things I heard people say when I was young, so I believed it. While he isn't what I consider a real man for abusing a woman, it doesn't mean he's a weakling with a complex. He may be a physically strong man, who may just have a bad temper or attitude and / or other psychological issues. As history has shown, he could be a martial arts or fighting professional, or even a famous entertainer. Expertise or celebrity status doesn't stop him from being violent if that is what he chooses to do.

The man inclined to domestic violence, or who is "on the edge", could be any of the Plan characters. There's no mathematical formula for predetermining this. Just use common sense along with discernment, and read the signs. With some women, Plan A or B could be 'on the edge' and he's sometimes still in the same Plan category.

Always A Blameless Victim?

It may sound as if I speak about women being abused who are only guilty of not cutting off such a relationship. In reality though, there are some cases in which women create or instigate the violence. Some, while they may not acknowledge it, feel that a man's physical domination over them is the way it's supposed to be. Perhaps it has been all they've known in the relationships they've seen close to them. Others may provoke their man to frustrate and agitate him because they want to get back at him for some reason. Still others may do it in order to make the man hit her, and then get him into legal trouble. In any case, it's just not the way to handle things. This woman who does this needs professional counseling. Some women will challenge a man, insult his manhood, stand in his way when he seeks to leave, and sometimes even attack him first. She may say the most insulting things; things that will cut him deeply. For a man who is involved with a woman like this, he should consider either helping her to get help to improve the situation, or weigh the option of leaving. If he doesn't, he could either find himself in trouble with the law by his reaction or continue to be a victim himself.

At times violence may happen due to a partner's infidelity. This still does not justify violence, but there are people who may even flaunt having another partner and say hurtful things to the significant other. Before the relationship gets to this point, good judgment is needed and it may help to seek out spiritual advice or a mature mentor if professional advice is not available.

Chapter 6:

Nightmare On Your Street

Chapter 6:
Nightmare On
Your Street

This chapter is designed to tell you true stories that will show you the seriousness of domestic violence and the people who perpetrate it. If it takes fear to help women see that this is something to avoid like the plague, then be fearful. Again, I speak about women because they are the largest victimized group, and they need to read the signs as mentioned in the previous chapter. For men who are victims of abuse, the same basic message applies: Watch for the signs early before getting into the relationship. If already involved, seek professional help. If the situation can't be resolved in a sensible way and time frame, then consider exit options.

Enough Is Enough...Too Late

There was a young lady, who was very beautiful, she had a super figure, and was very smart in school. She got involved with a guy right out of high school, married, and was with him for a number of years. During the relationship he was very abusive and even stabbed her. She recovered and didn't press charges. She took him back. Later, while enduring more abuse, he stabbed her again. She recovered again, didn't press charges, and took him back again. Finally after the abuse continued, she decided to divorce and end it for all. He asked her to meet him to arrange concluding their business matters. When she did, he shot her to death. No doubt she didn't leave in the beginning because she hoped things would improve.

Still Not Enough

Once, when I was about thirteen or fourteen, two of my brothers and I were at an older associate's house. We'll call him Joe. His girlfriend was there, sitting on the couch trying to look cute for him with her makeup and tight jeans on. She didn't talk much. He playfully hit her with his belt to get a reaction from her and to show off in front of us. He did it a few more times, harder than the first. She told him to stop, as we did. Then, Joe took the belt, wrapped it around her neck, and started dragging her from one side of the couch to the other with a sadistic laugh. We had never seen this before. We grabbed him to take the pressure off of the belt and wrestled to stop him. When we stopped him, he continued to laugh. She jumped up with tears in her eyes, and cursed him as she stormed out of the door. As we scolded him, he said repeatedly, "She'll be back. Watch, she'll be back." Less than thirty minutes later, she walked back in the door and sat on the couch, pouting like a child with her arms folded. We left in shock, as they were about to have sex.

Chapter 6: Nightmare On Your Street

ER Can't Save

A young lady was in an abusive relationship, and at some point decided to leave. I don't have all of the details, but eventually she and her father found themselves fleeing from the abuser in an automobile. He chased them at a high speed, and they drove to a hospital. They ran into the ER section of the hospital seeking to evade him and get help. The perpetrator ran in after them and shot them both. Even in the ER itself, the lives of the two could not be saved.

My Problem: Family Fate

An angry man decided to do the ultimate to hurt his ex. He shot their children, her mother, and her sister. He also shot her. To my understanding, she survived but the family did not.

This is something that **everyone** who dates must **seriously** consider. Who you are involved with could very easily affect those you love. "No man is an island." Some people say, *"It's my life. I date who I choose."* While this may be true, remember that people inclined to violence in this way could try to reach out to what hurts you the most. Those family members mentioned above that died weren't dating the perpetrator. They may have been against it from the very beginning, but now, just because of being close to the abused, they also had to suffer. Don't put your loved ones through this. If not for yourself, think of them. Make wise decisions, and _stay by them._

Plan B, C, & D
The Men Women Choose When They Don't Have What They *Really* Want!

My Doubt, My Grandchild

One mother was told by her daughter that the stepfather was sexually abusing her. The mother didn't believe her. Eventually the daughter showed the mother a video where the stepfather recorded the abuse. The mother killed the stepfather in his sleep. It turned out that the daughter was pregnant by him.

No Means NO...Right?

One young lady was in a relationship and her boyfriend knew she wanted to remain celibate at this time. He was in agreement with this in the beginning. She saw signs of abusive tendencies in the relationship, but downplayed them. Eventually, he raped her. She felt guilt from some part she must have played in this, and stayed with him. He eventually raped her a second time.

Too Far To Quit Now. Hurry Up and Die!

Poor decisions certainly are not limited to the young or a specific social class. One lady (Jane) was afraid of her second husband. She feared that he would kill her and her children and constantly hid anything sharp in the house.

After that marriage, her third was also bad. In the beginning her third husband (Joe) would spend time with the kids and give Jane money for them all to buy things. After the wedding, it all stopped. A month after the wedding she knew it was the wrong decision. He was very abusive verbally and mentally and mean spirited

70

Chapter 6: Nightmare On Your Street

even to the children. He had told her he only had one child, yet she later found that was a lie. He was guilty of credit fraud, shady business practices and I.D. theft (even stealing his own son's identity). Jane was married twice before and thought if she left this husband, "What would people think?" She also feared leaving him sick with diabetes, leaving her familiar surroundings and being back on her own, and she feared him physically and the fact that he owned a riffle.

She was 33 when they met, 35 when they married. She had a bachelor's degree when they met and she later got her master's degree. She was drawn to him by the idea of being financially stable, her love of the idea of being in love, and not wanting to be promiscuous if she wasn't married. Her self esteem was low and so she settled, even after seeing certain signs. She was a nurse's aid and due to her nurturing nature, she wanted to "save" him so to speak.

Her advice to women or potential victims: DON'T IGNORE THE SIGNALS. Her minister, counselors, and others would reason with her to stay. They'd say, "He's really sick, and doesn't have much longer to live anyway." Jane feels he may have sought her out for a connection to her medical insurance. They were married for 12 years, and separated four times. At times she would stand in the doorway watching him sleep and wishing he was dead. When she saw him move, she was disappointed. He died a slow and painful death.

[Note: This is expressed from Jane's account of the experience.]
Let's make good decisions that won't put us in these situations.

Plan B, C, & D
The Men Women Choose When They Don't Have What They *Really* Want!

The following information is taken from the National Domestic Violence Hotline website, www.ndvh.org. They have a great deal of information and resources for victims. Please visit their site for more information, or call 1 (800) 799-SAFE (7233).

National Statistics

The National Domestic Violence Hotline has received more than 1,000,000 calls for assistance since February 1996. – *National Domestic Violence Hotline, December 2004*

- Nearly one-third of American women (31 percent) report being physically or sexually abused by a husband or boyfriend at some point in their lives. – *Commonwealth Fund survey, 1998*

- It is estimated that 503,485 women are stalked by an intimate partner each year in the United States. – National Institute of Justice, July 2000

- Estimates range from 960,000 incidents of violence against a current or former spouse, boyfriend, or girlfriend each year to 4 million women who are physically abused by their husbands or live-in partners each year. – *Violence by Intimates: Analysis of Data on Crimes by Current or Former Spouses, Boyfriends, and Girlfriends, U.S. Department of Justice, March, 1998*

- Studies show that child abuse occurs in 30-60% of family violence cases that involve families with children. – *"The overlap between child maltreatment*

Chapter 6: Nightmare On Your Street

and woman battering." J.L. Edleson, Violence Against Women, February, 1999

• While women are less likely than men to be victims of violent crimes overall, women are 5 to 8 times more likely than men to be victimized by an intimate partner. *– Violence by Intimates: Analysis of Data on Crimes by Current or Former Spouses, Boyfriends, and Girlfriends, U.S. Department of Justice, March, 1998*

• Violence by an intimate partner accounts for about 21% of violent crime experienced by women and about 2 % of the violence experienced by men. *– Violence by Intimates: Analysis of Data on Crimes by Current or Former Spouses, Boyfriends, and Girlfriends, U.S. Department of Justice, March, 1998*

• In 92% of all domestic violence incidents, crimes are committed by men against women. *– Violence Against Women, Bureau of Justice Statistics, U.S. Department of Justice, January, 1994*

• Of women who reported being raped and/or physically assaulted since the age of 18, three quarters (76 percent) were victimized by a current or former husband, cohabitating partner, date or boyfriend. *– Prevalence Incidence, and Consequences of Violence Against Women: Findings from the National Violence Against Women Survey, U.S. Department of Justice, November, 1998*

• In 1994, women separated from their spouses had a victimization rate 1 1/2 times higher than separated men, divorced men, or divorced women. – *Sex Differences in Violent Victimization, 1994, U.S. Department of Justice, September, 1997*

- In 1996, among all female murder victims in the U.S., 30% were slain by their husbands or boyfriends. – *Uniform Crime Reports of the U.S. 1996, Federal Bureau of Investigation, 1996*

- 31,260 women were murdered

  by an intimate from 1976-1996. – *Violence by Intimates: Analysis of Data on Crimes by Current or Former Spouses, Boyfriends, and Girlfriends, U.S. Department of Justice, March, 1998*

- A child's exposure to the father abusing the mother is the strongest risk factor for transmitting violent behavior from one generation to the next. – *Report of the American Psychological Association Presidential Task Force on Violence and the Family, APA, 1996*

- Forty percent of teenage girls age 14 to 17 report knowing someone

  their age who has been hit or beaten by a boyfriend. – *Children Now/Kaiser Permanente poll, December, 1995*

- Females accounted for 39% of the hospital emergency department visits for violence-related injuries

Chapter 6: Nightmare On Your Street

in 1994 but 84% of the persons treated for injuries inflicted by intimates.– *Violence by Intimates: Analysis of Data on Crimes by Current or Former Spouses, Boyfriends, and Girlfriends, U.S. Department of Justice, March, 1998*

- Family violence costs the nation from $5 to $10 billion annually in medical expenses, police and court costs, shelters and foster care, sick leave, absenteeism, and non-productivity. – *Medical News, American Medical Association, January, 1992*

- Husbands and boyfriends commit 13,000 acts of violence against women in the workplace every year.– *Violence and Theft in the Workplace, U.S. Department of Justice, July, 1994*

- The majority of welfare recipients have experienced domestic abuse in their adult lives and a high percentage are currently abused. – *Trapped by Poverty, Trapped by Abuse: New Evidence Documenting the Relationship Between Domestic Violence and Welfare, The Taylor Institute, April, 1997*

1. One in five female high school students reports being physically or sexually abused by a dating partner. – *Massachusetts Youth Risk Behavior Survey (YRBS), August 2001*

Plan B, C, & D
The Men Women Choose When They Don't Have What They *Really* Want!

To find help in your state, call the National Domestic Violence Hotline. To find out more information about domestic violence in your state, call or write to one of the following state coalitions.

Alabama Coalition Against Domestic Violence P.O. Box 4762 Montgomery, AL 36101 Phone: 334-832-4842 FAX: 334-832-4803 http://www.azcadv.org	Alaska Network on Domestic Violence and Sexual Assault 130 Seward, Suite 209 Juneau, Alaska 99801 (907) 586-3650 http://www.andvsa.org
Arizona Coalition Against Domestic Violence 100 West Camelback Street, Suite 109 Phoenix, AZ 85013 Phone: 602-279-2900 FAX: 602-279-2980 www.azacadv.org	Arkansas Coalition Against Domestic Violence #1 Sheriff Lane, Suite C North Little Rock, AR 72114 Phone: 501-812-0571 FAX: 501-812-0578
California Alliance Against Domestic Violence 926 J Street, Suite 1000 Sacramento CA 95814 Telephone 916-444-7163 or 800-524-4765	California Alliance Against Domestic Violence - Southern Office 8929 S. Sepulveda Blvd., Suite 520

Chapter 6: Nightmare On Your Street

Fax 916-444-7165 e-mail caadv@cwo.com http://www.caadv.org	Los Angeles CA 90045-3605 Telephone 310-649-3953 Fax 310-649-2479 Return to top
Statewide California Coalition for Battered Women 3711 Long Beach Blvd., #718 Long Beach, CA 90807 Telephone: 562/981-1202 Fax: 981-3202 Toll-free: 888/722-2952 e-mail: sccbw@sccbw.org	Colorado Coalition Against Domestic Violence P.O. Box 18902 Denver, CO 80218 Phone: 303-831-9632 FAX: 303-832-7067
Connecticut Coalition Against Domestic Violence 106 Pitken Street East Hartford, CT 06108 860-282-7899 FAX: 860-282-7892 800-281-1481 (In State) 888-774-2900 (In State Hotline)	D. C. Coalition Against Domestic Violence 513 U Street, NW Washington, DC 20001 202-387-5630 (phone) 202-387-5684 (fax) dccadv@aol.com (email)
Delaware Coalition Against Domestic Violence 100 West 10th Street, Suite 703 Wilmington, DE 19801 Phone: 302-658-2958	Florida Coalition Against Domestic Violence 308 E. Park Avenue Tallahassee, FL 32301 (850) 425-2749

Plan B, C, & D
The Men Women Choose When They Don't Have What They *Really* Want!

FAX: 302-658-5049 **Return to top**	Fax: (850) 425-3091 TDD: (850) 621-4202 In-state: 800-500-1119
Georgia Coalition on Family Violence 3420 Norman Berry Drive Suite 280 Atlanta, GA 30354 Phone: 404-209-0280 FAX: 404-766-3800 800-334-2836 (In State Hotline)	Hawaii State Coalition Against Domestic Violence 98-939 Moanalua Road Aiea, HI 96701-5012 Phone: 808-486-5072 FAX: 808-486-5169
Idaho Coalition Against Sexual and Domestic Violence 815 Park Blvd., Suite 140 Boise, ID 83712 Phone: 208-384-0419 FAX: 208-331-0687 E-mail: domvio@micron.net	Illinois Coalition Against Domestic Violence 801 S. 11th St. Springfield, IL 62703 Phone: 217-789-2830 FAX: 217-789-1939 http://www.ilcadv.org
Indiana Coalition Against Domestic Violence 2511 E. 46th Street, Suite N-3 Indianapolis, IN 46205 TOLL-FREE: 800-332-7385 Phone: 317-543-3908 FAX: 317-377-7050	Iowa Coalition Against Domestic Violence 2603 Bell Avenue, Suite 100 Des Moines, IA 50321 Phone: 515-244-8028 FAX: 515-244-7417 In-State Hotline (Not

Chapter 6: Nightmare On Your Street

http://www.violenceresource.org Return to top	part of the Coalition) 800-942-0333 http://www.icadv.org
Kansas Coalition Against Sexual and Domestic Violence 220 SW 33rd Street, Suite 100 Topeka, KS 66611 Phone: 785-232-9784 FAX: 785-266-1874 http://www.kcsdv.org	Kentucky Domestic Violence Association P.O. Box 356 Frankfort, KY 40602 Phone: 502-695-2444 FAX: 502-695-2488 http://www.kdva.org
Louisiana Coalition Against Domestic Violence P.O. Box 77308 Baton Rouge, LA 70879 Phone: 222-752-1296 FAX: 222-751-8927 http://www.lcadv.org	Maine Coalition to End Domestic Violence 128 Main Street Bangor, ME 04401 Phone: 207-941-1194 FAX: 207-941-2327
Maryland Network Against Domestic Violence 6911 Laurel Bowie Road, Suite 309 Bowie, MD 20715 TOLL-FREE: 800-MD-HELPS Phone: 301-352-4574	Massachusetts Coalition Against Sexual Assault and Domestic Violence Jane Doe, Inc. 14 Beacon Street, Suite 507 Boston, MA 02108 Phone: 617-248-0922

Plan B, C, & D
The Men Women Choose When They Don't Have What They *Really* Want!

FAX: 301-809-0422 http://www.mnadv.org	FAX: 617-248-0902 **Return to top**
Michigan Coalition Against Domestic & Sexual Violence 3893 Okemos Road, Ste B2 Okemos MI 48864 ph: 517-347-7000 fax: 517-347-1377	Minnesota Coalition for Battered Women 450 North Syndicate Street, Suite 122 St. Paul, MN 55104 Phone: 612-646-6177 FAX: 612-646-1527 (800) 289-6177 http://www.mcbw.org
Mississippi State Coalition Against Domestic Violence P.O. Box 4703 Jackson, MS 39296-4703 TOLL-FREE: 800-898-3234 Phone: 601-981-9196 FAX: 601-981-2501 http://www.mcadv.org	Missouri Coalition Against Domestic Violence 415 East McCarty Jefferson City, MO 65101 Phone: 573-634-4161 FAX: 573-636-3728
Montana Coalition Against Domestic Violence P.O. Box 633 Helena, MT 59624 Phone: 406-443-7794	Nebraska Domestic Violence and Sexual Assault Coalition 825 M Street, Suite 404 Lincoln, NE 68508-2253 In-State Toll Free: 800-

Chapter 6: Nightmare On Your Street

FAX: 406-443-7818 Return to top	876-6238 Phone: 402-476-6256 FAX: 402-476-6806 http://www.ndvsac.org
Nevada Network Against Domestic Violence 100 West Grove Street, Suite 315 Reno, NV 89509 TOLL-FREE: 800-230-1955 Phone: 775-828-1115 FAX: 775-828-9911	New Hampshire Coalition Against Domestic and Sexual Violence P.O. Box 353 Concord, NH 03302-0353 In-State Toll Free: 800-852-3388 Phone: 603-224-8893 Fax: 603-228-6096 http://www.nhcadsv.org
New Jersey Coalition for Battered Women 2620 Whitehorse Hamilton Square Road Trenton, NJ 08690 TOLL-FREE: for Battered Lesbians: 800-224-0211 (in NJ only) In-State Toll Free: 800-572-7233	New Mexico State Coalition Against Domestic Violence 114 Oak NE Albuquerque, NM 87106 TOLL-FREE: 800-773-3645 (in NM Only) Phone: 505-246-9240 FAX: 505-246-9434

Plan B, C, & D
The Men Women Choose When They Don't Have What They *Really* Want!

Phone: 609-584-8107 FAX: 609-584-9750 http://www.nhcadsv.org	http://www.nmcadv.org Return to top
New York State Coalition Against Domestic Violence 79 Central Avenue Albany, NY 12206 TOLL-FREE: 800-942-6906 TOLL-FREE (Spanish): 800-942-6908 Phone: 518-432-4864 FAX: 518-463-3155 E-mail: nyscadv@aol.com http://www.nyscadv.org	North Carolina Coalition Against Domestic Violence 115 Market Street, Suite 400 Durham, NC 27707 Phone: 919-956-9124 FAX: 919-682-1449
North Dakota Council on Abused Women's Services State Networking Office 418 East Rosser Avenue, Suite 320 Bismarck, ND 58501-4046 TOLL-FREE: 800-472-2911 (In ND Only) Phone: 701-255-6240 FAX: 701-255-1904	Ohio Domestic Violence Network 4807 Evanswood Drive, Suite 201 Columbus, OH 43229 Toll Free: 800-934-9840 Phone: 614-781-9651 Fax: 614-781-9652 E-mail: info@odvn.org Website: www.odvn.org
Oklahoma Coalition Against	Oregon Coalition

Chapter 6: Nightmare On Your Street

Domestic Violence and Sexual Assault
2525 NW Expressway, Suite 101
Oklahoma City, OK 73112
phone 405-848-1815
fax 405-848-3469
TOLL FREE 1-800-522-7233

Return to top

Against Domestic and Sexual Violence
659 Cottage St NE
Salem, OR 97301
503-365-9644
503-566-7870 fax
E-mail:
ocadsv@teleport.com

http://www.ocadsv.com

Pennsylvania Coalition Against Domestic Violence/National Resource Center on Domestic Violence
6400 Flank Drive, Suite 1300
Harrisburg, PA 17112-2778
TOLL-FREE: 800-932-4632
Phone: 717-545-6400
FAX: 717-671-8149

http://www.pcadv.org

Rhode Island Coalition Against Domestic Violence
422 Post Road, Suite 202
Warwick, RI 02888
In-State TOLL-FREE: 800-494-8100
Phone: 401-467-9940
FAX: 401-467-9943

http://www.ricadv.org

South Carolina Coalition Against Domestic Violence & Sexual
Assault
P.O. Box 7776
Columbia, SC 29202-7776
TOLL-FREE: 800-260-9293

South Dakota Coalition Against Domestic Violence and Sexual
Assault
P.O. Box 141
Pierre, SD 57501
TOLL-FREE: 800-572-

Plan B, C, & D
The Men Women Choose When They Don't Have What They *Really* Want!

Phone: 803-750-1222 FAX: 803-750-1246 http://www.sccadvsa.org	9196 Phone: 605-945-0869 FAX: 605-945-0870 Return to top
Tennessee Coalition Against Domestic and Sexual Violence P.O. Box 120972 Nashville, TN 37212 Office: 615) 386-9406 Fax: (615) 383-2967 Toll Free Information Line: (800) 289-9018 (8 a.m. - 5 p.m. M-F) Statewide Domestic Violence and Child Abuse Hotline: (800) 356-6767 Email: tcadsv@telelink.net http://www.tcadsv.citysearch.com	Texas Council on Family Violence 8701 P.O. Box 16180 Austin, TX 78716 Phone: 512-794-1133 FAX: 512-794-1199 http://www.tcfv.org
Utah Domestic Violence Advisory Council 120 North 200 West, #319 Salt Lake City, UT 84103 TOLL-FREE in Utah: 800-897-LINK Phone: 801-538-4635	Vermont Network Against Domestic Violence and Sexual Assault P.O. Box 405 Montpelier, VT 05601 Phone: 802-223-1302

Chapter 6: Nightmare On Your Street

FAX: 801-538-4016	FAX: 802-223-6943
Virginians Against Domestic Violence 2850 Sandy Bay Road, Suite 101 Williamsburg, VA 23185 TOLL-FREE: 800-838-VADV Phone: 757-221-0990 FAX: 757-229-1553 Return to top	Washington State Coalition Against Domestic Violence 8645 Martin Way NE Suite 103 Lacey, WA 98516 360/407-0756 360/407-0761 FAX 360/407-0760 TTY http://www.wscadv.org
West Virginia Coalition Against Domestic Violence Elk Office Center 4710 Chimney Drive, Suite A Charleston, WV 25302 Phone: 304-965-3552 FAX: 304-965-3572 http://www.wvcadv.org	Wisconsin Coalition Against Domestic Violence 307 South Paterson, Suite 1 Madison, WI 53703 Phone: 608-255-0539 FAX: 608-255-3560 http://www.wcasa.org
Wyoming Coalition Against Domestic Violence and Sexual Assault P.O. Box 236 Laramie, WY 82073	U.S. Virgin Islands Women's Coalition of St. Croix

Plan B, C, & D
The Men Women Choose When They Don't Have What They *Really* Want!

Phone: 307-755-5481 FAX: 307-755-5482	Box 2734 St. Croix, VI 00822 Phone: 809-773-9272 Return to top
Women's Resource Center 8 Kongens GadeSt. Thomas, VI 00802 Phone: 809-722-2907	Coordinadora Paz para la Mujer, Inc Proyecto Coalicion Contra la Violencia Domestica P.O. Box 1007 RMS 108 San Juan, Puerto Rico 00919 Phone: 787-281-7579 Fax: 787-767-6843 Correo electronico: pazparalamujer@yunque.net
Comision Para Los Asuntos De La MujerBox 11382 Fernandez Juancus Station Santurce, Puerto Rico 00910 787-722-2907	

Chapter 6: Nightmare On Your Street

[End of ndvh.org information]

Sites that may be of assistance:

www.ndvh.org
http://abuse.com
http://www.abuse.com/domestic_violence/
http://batteredmenshelpline.org
http://www.ojp.usdoj.gov/ovc/help/dv.htm

PART 3:

CHANGE MY PLAN? HOW?

Chapter 7:

Plan D and C

Chapter 7:
Plan D and C

Let's first discuss **Plan D.** There are positive attributes in all Plans, but for Sue, the attributes of D are less desired. Women want a man they feel to be strong or capable; physically yes, but mentally and psychologically also. The bottom line: I think people should be themselves. Yet, if there is a part of you that you choose to change, do it because you want that change for yourself.

Manhood In Perspective

Before we talk about some changes you may choose to make, let me tell you about an experience of mine. I went out with a young lady for the first time, and we went to a rally arranged to keep the pursuit of justice going for a Black man murdered by a police officer. It was an emotional atmosphere. By the time the widow got up to speak, seeing her emotions and looking at her daughter and knowing it could have been me they were talking about and my daughter others were looking at, I shed a few tears! I couldn't prevent it, though I tried. My date didn't cry, but I couldn't help it. Did that make me weak? Though I preferred not to weep, I wasn't overly concerned about what anyone else thought. The experience of the atmosphere was profound to me, and

I'm confident in who I am. Even knowing he would resurrect Lazarus, Jesus cried at his death. So my male readers, it's not a matter of being in touch with your "feminine side." There's not one macho and one feminine side of you, but all of what we feel as humans are in the one man that we are. It's simply a human emotion. The feminine side expression is one thing that makes men think we can't express emotion sometimes. People's perception of what manliness is has been obscured. Love and compassion is not weak or feminine. Now that being said; I'm not saying a man should be overboard with it either. Balance is always good. If my experience that day makes me Plan D for a Sue, then so be it. Sue is not the kind of woman for me. (The young lady I went with and I are still cool, by the way!)

What You Can Do

Again, be yourself; but if you feel there are some changes you should make regarding Plan D traits, consider these: If you aren't fairly well built physically, exercise or go to the gym regularly. To attract what we want, we have to be willing to at least come a good part of the way ourselves. Study those who are strong in other ways that you admire, and see what you can do to develop some of those attributes. Read self help books, such as those from Anthony Robbins, Les Brown and the like. Learn how to be a better leader, without training to be a tyrant. Develop a good comfort level with making decisions quickly when possible, because a decisive man receives a higher level of respect from a woman. Communication is critical to a friendship / relationship, so learn how to express yourself, and when to listen.

Chapter 7: Plan D and C

There's a time for everything.

Plan D is the nice guy, but remember that while it's good to be kind, women (even women who are not a Sue) don't want a pushover. A balance of kindness, firmness (when needed), and control of the order of things is needed. Keyword: balance. Don't be a jellyfish, and don't be a bull.

If you call someone from time to time and they never call you first or return your calls, leave them alone. You can't make anyone want your company, so "don't throw your pearls to swine." Do the things mentioned above, and if they still view you as a convenience to them, if it really matters to you, then tell them how you feel about your friendship and be bold about what you'd like to happen or change. Sometimes people look over others because they were never outspoken enough to say what they really wanted. If they never give you the respect or regard that *everyone* should receive, then let it go. You can't change *anyone* except yourself. If they schedule dates with you and cancel more than once without reasonable notice or cause, CUT THEM OFF!!! That's just my advice, because if you keep letting it happen then they won't respect you. You may even choose to cut it off if it happens once, but you have to decide that, along with what you call "reasonable cause." If you, like me, have a low patience for this then it may be good to mention this very early on.

If they try to keep you on standby, implying they "may call you later" or they "may be able to get together" at a certain time, tell them the two of you will have to plan for another time so as not to hold up your time if it can't be confirmed. If you're in the process of changing your Plan category or how you do things, give them fair notice.

Plan B, C, & D
The Men Women Choose When They Don't Have What They *Really* Want!

When you make plans, you may want to tell them, "I'll keep that time as we scheduled, but if you can't make it for any reason please let me know in a reasonable time." That conveys the thought that your time is valuable and is to be respected. A 24-hour notice seems reasonable to me (unless your plans involved something that required advance planning like going out of town). Still you also want to give the other person the opportunity to be a responsible adult, so don't give them a set cancellation hour. Then, IF it matters to her then she'll want to reschedule and get her act together, seeing you now have a higher regard for yourself. If you don't respect yourself, no one else will. Ladies, maybe you want to get together with your date, but something legitimate came up. If you really do want to see him, let him know you do. If you don't make that clear, he may feel you're blowing him off and it can hinder your good chemistry. Generally speaking though, you can tell when someone puts you in 'tenth priority'. If it's not a matter of things that are out of their control or legitimate obligations, (children, religious, work, etc.) they'll let you know in advance they want to spend time with you when possible. Do you usually get their voicemail, with it taking a day or more to return your call, especially when you call on the weekend? I recently heard someone on the radio (just before I turned the station) ask a psychic if a guy was really into her. You don't need a psychic to tell you if someone is into you, though reading the book *He's Just Not That Into You* by Greg Behrendt and Liz Tuccillo may be helpful, because sometimes we're clueless as to just how clueless we really are. From what I've heard of the book, much of the information can be applied to females by male readers also.

Chapter 7: Plan D and C

Here's another thing. I find that when I enjoy someone's conversation or company, I could talk all night. This could be a mistake, depending on the other person's vibe. If you have a good vibe, you can tell that you're both enjoying the conversation. If they're as thrilled to be talking that long or late as you, then great, but never over extend yourself to the point that the other person is ready to part, and you're holding them up. It could make them a bit more hesitant to call or be in your company, especially if it's late. NEVER make them feel like, "Oh, it's him (or her)!" Even if you want to talk longer or stay with them longer, be conscious of the other person and tear away before they lose interest. Sometimes it's good to make them wish you'd talk or stay in their company longer, and miss you when you go. Again, there's a time for everything, but even if you're not the first to end the time, DON'T MAKE THEM TIRE OF YOU!

For **Plan C**, he may choose to become a Plan A or B for the appeal of being Sue's main choice or her choice for sex. Still, C has some good qualities, so I would say don't loose that. C may have a decent job and have good basic values. I feel C may be able to get some insight from the other Plans, but may have some degree of their characteristics already. For women more discerning than Sue, C or D may very well be Plan A.

Plan B, C, & D
The Men Women Choose When They Don't Have What They *Really* Want!

Interracial Inspiration

In the African American community, I've heard of Plans C and D being inclined to date interracially because of their being tired of the shallow Sues in the community, so they find themselves looking for change in other places. While I cannot speak on this issue with my own experience, they sometimes speak of women from other races not being as concerned about material things as a prerequisite to a relationship or spending time. This is by no means a character description of Plans C and D, but describes the reasoning of some. Many feel that the economic challenges in the Black community create a growing divide between Black men and Black women. I agree, and believe that there is becoming more of an emphasis on a man's status than his character with many women. I believe that this is the case with women in general, but I am personally most familiar with this happening in the Black community. The same women who will overlook a man because he's not their Plan A, will talk about him severely when she sees him with a woman of another race (especially if she's White). Afterwards, that same woman (in some cases) could even find *herself* in an interracial relationship at some point.

Plan A may date interracially due to his means giving him access to different communities, cultures, events and people, and / or his feeling that he 'owes it to himself.' Some Black people who have low self esteem (even if they don't recognize it as such) feel that dating someone White is a step upward. Sometimes they even choose a White partner to make their children, according to their view, more attractive. I think this low self image is

Chapter 7: Plan D and C

unfortunate.

Sue (African American or any other nationality) may date interracially in her pursuit of resources. Other women (Black or otherwise) may do so in the interest of a relationship of some kind, without resources being the main factor. It could be due to past experiences, a lack of compatible options, or they may just have other preferences. These examples of interracial dating are not all inclusive, however, because of course there are couples that just happen to meet, learn and love each other for no other reason. Just as there are various personalities and views in every community, so there are various circumstances as well.

Chapter 8:

Becoming Plan B?

Chapter 8:
Becoming Plan B?

Much of Plan B involves a sexual relationship with Sue. Another aspect of B is the fact that he will not or cannot commit. That should be one of the easiest parts of that Plan; just be truthful that you will not commit if that's your choice. Let her know up front. Easier said than done, right? Often men won't do that because they want to have their way and it may require her thinking he plans to develop a long-term relationship with her. Being truthful is the best way, because there are people whose lifestyle works with yours. Yet since people will be people despite any contrary admonition, women have to be discerning to identify whom they're dealing with.

Keep It Real

A rough or bad boy image that B may be associated with is not something that I would suggest someone don unnaturally. If that's not your way, don't fake it. It could be an embarrassment to you to try and I believe it's unnecessary. Some women like certain kind of men that just are *not who you are.* You can't be all things to all, so find those who seek who you are.

Plan B could be someone she feels is a strong or respectable man. There are various ways to exhibit strength and merit respect. Speak your mind and work on building up your confidence if you need to. You don't have to be cruel, rude, or tacky about it, but people respect when you're able to speak up for what you feel even if it's not the popular thing to say.

Whether or not you are chosen to be her choice as a partner I believe is largely based on your chemistry (vibe). That is often the fuel for performance psychologically and physically.

Can Your S.O. Have The Plan B Effect?

Regarding someone already in a relationship, you may want to become more of a sexual person to your S.O. (significant other). I do believe that in most cases, the heightened level of intimacy she may enjoy or imagine with a Plan B can be experienced and surpassed in a committed relationship. For one, if she has someone compatible who can complement her, she can groom her thinking so that she knows she doesn't have to reach out into wonderland to feel the way she wants to, but can work with her partner to develop this level. Also, her partner can work on being more sexual. Many times in the routine of work and life, we see the shell of our partner, and the intimate thoughts of them are in the back room of our mind until we've rested, finished our daily routines and it's time to bring it out. We need to be able to see all or most of our partner's deeper attributes at any given time, and be able to convert into the passionate partner more quickly than we do. This doesn't always require sex to be involved to do this. It can be accomplished by verbal expressions, body language, or other things. We need to be standing by, constantly ready to handle any of our partner's needs. Outsourcing is not an option!

Chapter 9:

The Coveted A

Chapter 9:
The Coveted A

For men who want to be Plan A, my first thought is make yourself a great catch from within, then work externally. **Again my disclaimer: I am not a financial planner, and am not qualified to give financial advice. For financial advice, see a qualified professional. Any options discussed in this book are just that, options that can be discussed with qualified professionals to determine what is best for you.** When it comes to money, there are many things that can be done to improve your situation. I ONLY recommend the legal ways! Our prisons and cemeteries are crowded enough.

Mental And Financial Groundwork

Here are a few considerations if you're starting from zero: If you don't have a job, get one or two (if finances require that immediately). Work smart and diligently, even if in the beginning you're making low wages. Move up in the ranks of management, and <u>keep yourself as debt free as possible.</u> When you get a chunk of money; from a bonus, tax return, insurance claim, etc., don't just think of where you can spend it, but how you can invest in a business or something that will make it reproduce. Save money and invest in a Roth IRA, 401k or money market account. Don't know how? Ask your HR department at work or a bank representative. With your regular income, the ideal goal to strive for is to save / invest at least ten percent of your paycheck (of the gross if possible), use ten percent for contributions / to help others, and live off of the rest. If you can't do that now, consider how you can generate more revenue and cut back expenses to get you closer to the goal. Learn to be, not good, but great at something where you can eventually start your own business.   It should be something you really like or love doing. If you're not passionate about it—the kind of passion that keeps you up late at night to work on it on your own initiative—then you may quit at the first sign of difficulty and you may not be that good at it anyway. Success is not a coincidence; it's a process. Develop and maintain the "I'm on a mission" mindset. Your subconscious mind knows when you've really bought into something, and when you're bluffing. You can't fool it. Once it knows you're really serious, it goes to work for you, along with many supportive people who have respect for someone pursuing their goals. Don't just flirt with the idea of success; marry it and make it happen.

Take classes and attend seminars based on your business interests, <u>keep your credit excellent</u>, and remember your attitude and personality can sell you better than any skill you learn. It's not about how life is treating you; how are *you* treating *life?* Keep in mind that while you may have a right to express your individuality by your grooming and appearance, it will affect your marketability and options in many ways; for better or worse.

Chapter 9: The Coveted A

Go to school to get training in a field currently in demand; create a product or think of a service that's needed which you could provide. With a good plan, diligence and patience, you'll greatly improve your financial status. Plan well. Wishful thinking is not a good success strategy. Watch and even record how you spend or waste your time. If you don't love and cherish your time, you don't cherish life, because time is life. *We are the culmination of our investment of time,* so be sure to invest time feeding your mind productive food. Good seeds can't grow in unfertile soil. Make your mind fertile soil, and when the good seeds of opportunity come, your growth will be amazing. Read business and productivity books, magazines and articles. (*Rich Dad Poor Dad* by Robert Kiyosaki, *As A Man Thinketh* by James Allen and Florence S. Chinn's *The Game of Life and How To Play It* are _must_ reads). I am always in the process of reading a book. When I finish one, I start a new one. Listen to self help CDs while you drive or ride the train or bus.

Get Help

This is important also: Get a mentor to help you stay focused in the right direction. When you do, you need to be serious about your goals (make sure they're written down with completion times by each one). If you're not serious, then the mentor won't let you waste their time.

Be smart about your business. With any legal matter you have, consult an attorney to have them review the agreements. Can't afford it? You can. Get a pre-paid legal plan where they provide many free services such as contract review and unlimited phone

109

consultations. I pay $17 per month for my legal plan. Some include drafting a will for you at no extra charge. We all need a will. If more of our ancestors bought the right life insurance and had a will, then many broke people would be Plan A right now. There's more financial planning to know that goes along with a will and insurance, so become financially literate to plan properly and get legal insurance to help your status now and your family later.

Already Shining?

Now, for guys who are A's, many of you hate women to pursue you for your money. The rest may not mind, glad to have the privileges money brings. For those who hate the motive of pursuit, make sure you're not adding fuel to the problem. Is your status, accomplishments, or connections a part of your early conversation? Many are happy to show their car (or car key), talk about what they do (which may generate or require a lot of money) or talk about where they've been to impress others. Then, when they catch the attention of women who seek the means they have, they complain about being chased for the wrong reason or being used. Use good judgment. Don't put yourself in that situation. Women take it that you're going to use that money to benefit them, so to pursue you for that reason is alright with you. Whatever happened to character? Having it to acquire closeness, or having it to recognize someone else having it?

Sue really wants to be taken care of or decorated materially. There's nothing wrong with wanting nice things. How much better though, to be self sufficient and

Chapter 9: The Coveted A

learn to take care of yourself! Then, you don't have to worry about the control factor of someone who can pull the plug at any given time.

To PRE, or Not To PRE...

This is a very controversial issue, but I strongly believe in prenuptial agreements. I think men and women alike who have strong assets or resources should push for that, but not only them. Some people have little or nothing now, but will come into a prosperous situation later. Not only that, but as regards children, how will they be cared for? The father may want and be worthy of joint custody, but unless the mother agrees, he may only be given visitation rights. "Visitation of your own child." It sounds a lot like one of you are incarcerated. What happens then if one of the parents chooses to move out of town? Prenuptial agreements can address how all of that could be handled. I'm told, however, regarding an agreement involving unborn children, a judge may not enforce terms of custody and visitation. *Supposedly,* upon marriage it's naturally assumed there will be joint custody in the event of a divorce, but during the divorce one parent usually assumes more of the primary care responsibilities. Based on that, the judge awards the primary custody to that parent. Consult a qualified family law attorney for advice in this matter.

I believe if the two people in a relationship can agree on arrangements in a reasonable manner, they should determine them, not a judge. Yet if you can't agree on those things while you're in your state of love and harmony, what makes you think you'll have a judgment you think is fair later? Contrary to many people's objection with prenups, it's not predetermining failure, and doesn't have to mean there's a lack of love or trust. It's just foreknowledge that should the worse scenario happen, you have mutually controlled circumstances. There are people who already have it decided in their mind that if they found their mate being unfaithful, they will kill them. Not that you plan to be unfaithful at all, but wouldn't you want to know up front if your partner felt that way? That may sound like an extreme example, but just the same, if you do divorce for any reason, it's tough to find out then that circumstances in your life could be adversely affected because you didn't know your spouse would handle things the way they are, or even that the judge would rule the way they did. You don't plan to have an accident each day you drive, but you better keep your insurance current. Marriage is personal, but if you think you can separate business matters from it, you may be in for a rude awakening.

If you decide to do the prenup, be sure both parties have their own lawyer present when you sign. I heard of a case with a celebrity who had a lawyer there but his wife didn't, so at the divorce the judge ruled the agreement was unenforceable. She walked away with many, many millions!

PART 4:

THE BOTTOM LINE

Chapter 10:

The Vibe

Chapter 10:
The Vibe

What It's Like; And What It's Not

So many of the ills of dating could be avoided if we did more to make sure that we have the right vibe (connection or chemistry) with the person before taking it to the next step. If you're honest with yourself, many times we can tell at the initial meeting if there's a vibe; a warm "this feels good" feeling. The problem is, many times you've made up in your mind to talk to someone, usually due to physical attraction or maybe you just feel that person is into you. Then, even if you don't feel a connection with them, you continue because you say, "Well I've stepped out there so I might as well keep going." NEVER DO THIS. You don't *have* to give someone your number, or even keep up a conversation if along the way you feel it isn't for you. Most of us have been guilty of this at some point. You *should* feel like, *"Yeah, I think this is working out, I'm glad we've met."* If it's hum-drum or there's no flow, maybe you're trying to "get in where you don't fit in". Someone could be having a rough day, so take all things into consideration while you use practical judgment. And if you feel you're not yourself or you're in a social funk, why not say so to let the person you're encountering know it's not due to your view of them.

Plan B, C, & D
The Men Women Choose When They Don't Have What They *Really* Want!

Again, we have to be observant and honest with ourselves regarding what we want and who we're dealing with. This can be the start of someone occupying your time, and possibly your body and life; so make sure it fits, you with them and them with you. As you date someone you consider for a relationship, your expectations should be higher than those for a 'hang out' associate. You look deeper into your compatibility and the fiber of their character. As for you, can they really see who you are, the layers of your depth? When they look at you, do they see only what everyone else can see; or can they see, feel, and connect with your spirit? That's the 'you' that matters more than any other part of you. Not everyone has the need for this kind of intimacy, however. For some people if you get along well and do your role in the relationship they're fine. But whatever your needs are, be sure to fill them when it's time, not just in a physical way, but spiritually. Fill your soul.

It is true that sometimes you can seem to have a good vibe with someone and they turn out to be less than genuine. The person can act as though they're totally into you, and then drop off. Maybe they want to be constantly chased, or they just have too much going on to follow up with you. Even though you may be meeting and even dating other people, if you're interested in someone, slow down. Take the time to learn enough about them to see if they're someone you want to spend time with. If you just put them in a large pool of people you've met and numbers you've gathered, then you're likely just wasting time. If you only make time to call every blue moon, you may never get any value from their friendship. If you're not interested in taking some time to see what that person is like, then why waste your time or

Chapter 10: The Vibe

theirs by exchanging numbers?

Warning!

ALWAYS, ALWAYS, ALWAYS LISTEN TO THAT LITTLE VOICE IN YOUR HEAD!!! It may not hurt to look into why you get a negative vibe about someone sometimes, if you do so from a cautious distance, but at other times you may need to just cut it off immediately if the vibe is of that nature. If you don't feel you can trust someone, respect your feelings and don't disregard that vibe. This is a chapter that talks about making good decisions before getting yourself into a regretful situation. If you don't have confidence about a person's character, consider the pace in which you're moving or seriously consider if you want to go anywhere at all. Watch for the yellow and red flags.

Regarding the vibe and listening to that little voice, so many women now are concerned about bisexual men on the down-low, and understandably so. Not only are men who have sex with men the largest carriers of HIV / AIDS in this country, but simply put, a heterosexual woman wants a straight, heterosexual man. It has created a lot of paranoia in women, but also in heterosexual men trying to determine who's in their proximity, sometimes offending other heterosexual men by their undue suspicion.

I've heard on a radio show that some men tell women of their bisexuality, and some women (sometimes bisexual themselves) accept this. If the woman chooses to accept this, then the choice (and all that's involved with it) is hers. At least there are a few out there who have enough ethics to give her a choice. Most, however, are dishonest about it to prevent rejection. It's very unfortunate that people deceive others into having a relationship on false grounds. It's selfish and wrong in every way. But ladies, if you're observant and prayerful, not in denial and just determined to have someone, many times you can discern things *before* you catch him in a life shattering act, or find something of his that doesn't make sense. Stay conscious. I say it again, watch and listen for the yellow and red flags, and make sure you have open communication. If he lies about his sexuality, generally if he talks enough you'll find something that strikes your spirit. If he's not that open, then you need to understand why. Maybe that's just him, or maybe there are specific things he's not willing to share. His lack of openness can also help you determine the depth of your relationship.

What's It Gonna Be?

So many unnecessary games are played when dating. We go through rituals and foreplay of custom, when we really usually want one (occasionally two) of three things: (1) Sex (2) a relationship (3) a friendship. Of course the relationship usually comes with the sexual ties. Often, the friendship and sexual ties are separate, but occasionally people want them together. Whether you say it this way or not, they're all a form of a relationship, formally or informally. With a friendship, if feelings get involved or it gets physical, someone will grow attached, jealousy will exist, and you will act out what you deny in title. Though one or both parties may resist the formality, it'll usually either grow towards an "official" relationship or it will sooner or later crumble. It's

Chapter 10: The Vibe

human nature. (Although some people keep an informal relationship going for many years.)

Get it out in the open what it is you want. It doesn't have to be done or said in a crude way. While people won't always agree with your views or want the same things as you, they will usually respect your honesty.

No Nonsense Dating

Many people hold information about themselves close, like cards in a card game. There are things that should come in time; yet there is basic information that could let each person know some deciding factors, which I think should be discussed on the first date or first lengthy conversation. Information such as (the truth about) your relationship status, and what you're interested in regarding dating (commitment, casual, friendship open to a relationship, etc.). Also, any other likely 'show stopper' info, so you can put it on the table and avoid wasting time and feelings if it doesn't blend with your date. Information such as how you feel about having children or stepchildren (if considering a relationship), if you are waiting for marriage to have sex, or if it's critical to you to have your relationship (or marriage) partner join your religious organization. I call it sharing and comparing notes. It's like a verbal condensed summary sheet of who you are, some top essentials on your must-have list, and maybe some examples of things that conflict with you or your objectives ("can't deal with" items). Use discernment on what you convey, however, because some people will deceitfully shape a false image of themselves around what you tell them about you, just to get to a certain result.

I think one problem with relationships is we often times don't talk openly about our differences or faults at the outset. If it's not conversation that's flattering, romantic, or building toward something greater, we tend to avoid it if it's a person we're attracted to. Then when a relationship develops and problems arise, we crash because we never knew all of the issues and whether or not we were willing or able to deal with them. Out of the thousands of people and personalities out there, the chances that you are talking to someone who won't blend with you are high. IT'S OK. Don't try to make it more than it is. Again, by being honest with yourself and the person you're dealing with, it contributes to a no nonsense dating experience that is good for both parties, saving wasted time and feelings.

The 4 Level Dialog—The Dating Communication System!

What if you could meet someone, and know right away how much they're attracted or interested in you? Many times you can meet a smiling face and yet they were not as interested as you thought, or maybe they were more interested than you realized. Maybe you learned the correct situation after opportunity was lost, or after getting turned down. The 4 Level Dialog is a way to communicate with someone you approach (or who approaches you) which gives you (or the other person) access to the level of communication that they (or you) choose. That communication can reveal the level of

Chapter 10: The Vibe

attraction or interest one has, and can express a willingness to go out on a future date, such as in level 3. For people like me who don't have a bold and captivating approach as first nature, this can not only be refreshing, but invaluable in a renewed social life.

Level 1 can only discuss or access level 1, level 2 can access 1 and 2, level 3 can access 1-3, and level 4 can access anything in levels 1-4. I'll identify the subject matter in each level, and then we'll discuss how the 4 Level Dialog operates. ***It is VERY important that the topics be kept in their proper levels, and that anyone using this dialog FOLLOW THE RULES!***

Level 1:
*I'm not interested, but thank you for your interest. Not to be taken offensively, I'm sure you're a great person but I have a different preference. You're free to talk about the weather, current events, or something else **non**-personal.*

Level 2:
I have initial interest. We can discuss our relationship status, our interests, and <u>general</u> get-to-know basics. Polite courtesies such as complimenting my appearance are fitting, but don't get graphic! You're only on first base.

Level 3:
I'm definitely interested. I'm impressed with you and I think you're my type. You can ask me out / I'd like to take you out on a date. The level of communication may deepen (but don't lose tact).

Plan B, C, & D
The Men Women Choose When They Don't Have What They *Really* Want!

Level 4:
(Level 4 is a highway—enter at your own risk!) I'm definitely interested in and / or am attracted to you and I'm willing to talk candidly with you. You can ask me about my likes and dislikes in personal matters, or whatever you want to talk about. Whether I choose to answer or not is still based on my discretion, but the topics are wide open. (Careful, this level is not for the bashful!)

****

Ok, so now we have the groundwork. This is not a robotic script which takes away from your style or individuality. It still allows you to carry on the type of conversation that's comfortable for you and your new acquaintance. This is a guide that helps people who know how it works, to cut through some of the wasted time and hassles of initially meeting. Some women talk to men they're not interested in because they don't want to hurt their feelings and don't know how to turn them away. *The 4 Level Dialog* alleviates that, and can also be instrumental as an icebreaker and in overcoming fear of rejection with those you want to talk to.

When a friend and I met, after talking for a few minutes about general get-to-know conversation (Level 2 or 3), she asked me about my credit. I felt it was very inappropriate. While that's something you should know about a prospect for marriage, I think that's a subject that should be developed over time. I think that's more of a Level 4 item, but if I don't even know if she's someone who I want to talk to after this moment, why do I need to discuss information about my credit? We later became

Chapter 10: The Vibe

friends and she apologized for asking about credit, but she had in mind a negative past experience.

You may do well to start at one level and work your way up to level 4. Not only will people have different levels of attraction, but people move at different speeds. Don't feel offended if you would have extended level 3 or 4, but you've been extended level 1 or 2. After conversation, you could be asked to step it up to a higher level, but of course that's up to the individuals involved. How do you start, and how do you move up?

It starts by both people being familiar with *The 4 Level Dialog (4LD)*. You're reading about the system now, so that's step one. Next, go to my website, www.PlanBCD.com to obtain an official, current 4LD pin along with information about events and social meeting locations. (The pin has a magnet back and won't damage clothes). When you attend an event listed and see someone with the pin, you know they're familiar with the system.

One person (male or female) sees someone they're interested in. Let's say it's you approaching someone. You approach and say something like this: "Hello—my name is _____. May I speak freely?" Their response may be; "Sure, free-2 (or level 2)" if that is their interest. Based on their response, you know just how interested they are in you, and where your conversation can and can't go.

When being approached, even if you're not interested you should always respond with courtesy even to extend level 1. This way, the person will less likely feel an embarrassing rejection that makes the dating scene dreadful for some, and you both can still have a successful experience. Level 1 says "...*You're free to talk about the weather, current events, or something else non-personal.*" This is because it's mainly in a social setting where mingling is expected, and a brief courteous chat can keep the atmosphere positive. Still, if you don't feel comfortable with the person at all or feel disrespected for some reason, then you don't have to extend even level 1, you can just say "No thank you." Use your discretion and common sense in all cases.

As far as escalating to a higher level after the initial meeting, you can use your own words for that, but if you choose to do so ask the other person if they're interested in doing so, IF you feel both of your comfort level has gotten to that point. If you take it upon yourself to shift gears, you may be imposing on the other person's comfort level and you could be in for rejection.

If someone does escalate without your consent, you can give them a caution phrase to put them back on track and continue the conversation if you choose. If they get off track again then you can give them a termination phrase to discontinue the conversation. You can even terminate it the first time if you choose. You can use your own words, or the following:

Cautionary—"The Jolt"
"I think things escalated—Let's stay on level _____."

Termination—"Clean Break"
"We're back off track, and we need to close here. Enjoy your evening."

Chapter 10: The Vibe

The Rules:

1. *Keep all subject matter on the proper 'levels' that have been extended.* Don't advance levels without consent of the person you're talking to.
2. *DON'T TAKE IT PERSONAL IF SOMEONE EXTENDS LEVEL 1 OR TERMINATES THE CONVERSATION.*
   There are many types of people in this big world, and no one fits everyone's type. Be a good sport, or don't play at all. If they use the termination "clean break" phrase, don't try to change their mind and engage them in further conversation. LET IT GO.
3. ***TELL THE TRUTH ABOUT YOUR RELATIONSHIP STATUS!!!***
   This is HUGE. There are those out there who don't care about your being involved with someone if that is your case, but for those whom it matters to, give them the chance to choose. Let's leave the drama out of this dialog and don't complicate things.
4. *Don't exaggerate your interests.* This rule is asking a LOT, but I think it's necessary. You don't owe anyone flattery, so if they're only a level 2, don't extend level 3, and so forth. If you're not interested in a relationship at this time with this person, it would be good to let them know. Then if you discuss attraction, it's understood where things are with the two of you, and the other person won't waste time pursuing it if they want more. This rule even sounds naive of me to suggest, because I know that many people are in

127

pursuit of their own interests and will lead someone on to get what they want, in fear of the truth hindering them. We need to start nurturing better relationships. This candidness can be a good start to doing that.

5. <u>Use good judgment and common sense in all cases.</u> If someone doesn't know how to take no, you may need to inform the facility's management, the police, and / or leave the facility. If you do leave, you may want to have security escort you to your vehicle. Be sure to be observant on your way out to make sure that you are not being followed. It's safer for women to have a friend go to single's events with them.

You can purchase invitations the size of business cards from my website, where you can write in the location, date and time of an event listed on the website. This will allow you to invite people who may or may not know about the 4LD but can go to the site to get more information, and hopefully meet you at the next event. If you see someone attractive you'd like to talk to but don't quite have the words, this event invitation along with the website can do much of the talking for you. Keep some invitations handy! The card also has a place for your contact information, so if the person is interested they can let you know if they plan to attend, or just contact you for further discussion. I will also have T-shirts available on the website. If you're wearing one (even if you're not at one of my single's / social events), don't be surprised if someone speaks to you in "The 4 Level Dialog"!

As the next chapter "Needs and Wants" shows, it can be challenging to find a match for various reasons. It is

Chapter 10: The Vibe

my hope that this dialog, along with these gatherings and invitations, will help people to meet and communicate more effectively. When you do meet, in all cases use sound judgment.

****

Beware of The Pride Ride

There's a critical bottleneck stage early in dating where the vibe is fragile and often breaks, or chokes out. In this case, I'm not referring to an instance where you see that you're not compatible and decide to keep on moving. Rather, a time when your unfamiliarity makes a certain level of communication awkward. It's like a "Pride Ride", because pride is often the factor in this breakdown of communication, or it could be due to one person's impatience. It's a time when you've gotten to know the other person to some small degree and enjoy being around them, yet something feeds your pride and messes it up! You have developed expectations in the person, whether reasonable or not. Somehow the expectations are not met, and rather than tell the person you want to see them or what's really on your mind, you "ride" on your pride, refuse to initiate or return phone calls, and just "ride out"! This is a true example of immaturity. Because you haven't established a deep relationship, you tell yourself it's ok to let it go. If you could just make it through this bottle neck period, maybe you could have something good.   This poor communication ethic sometimes carries over into relationships also, but for small issues, If you were in a relationship you would likely talk about the thing that's bothering you. But since you're not at that point yet, you don't try as hard. I'm not suggesting you should have the same determination as you would in a relationship, because you may not even know if the person is right for you yet. Still, if you fail to get to the other side of the bottle neck period, you could miss out on something you really want. Even though you hope your partner will be mature enough to handle this awkward time, you both are feeling each other out right now, so give allowance for them not fully knowing you and both of your imperfect human nature. If you want to see her / him, say so. If they're clamming up and starting to take the Pride Ride, tell them how you'd like to see things happen differently. Most of the time this "ride" comes from a person not wanting to put their feelings out and not have them reciprocated. Reassure your partner that you want to get through this bottle neck period and get to know them or continue to see them, if this is indeed the case. I think one of the biggest romantic tragedies is for two people who want to be with each other, to go separate ways and lose out due to pride, failed communication, or something trivial. You've got to be bold enough to make sure the other person knows exactly how you feel, so if it's not reciprocated then at least you've done your part.

Out of Sync

Some women try to control the dating process from early on. While it's necessary for her to determine when the timing is best for her to have sex, when she's ready, she sometimes expects him to read her right on cue and act on it right then. Regardless of his time table,

Chapter 10: The Vibe

if she's ready she feels he better be also. If he's not, she may question his sexuality, his intelligence if he doesn't pick up on a hint, or become frustrated that he's not more aggressive. I personally have not responded to hints or redirected the course of things if it was not what I wanted to do at that time. This can easily break things in the "Pride Ride" time frame. This will cause some women to think of the guy as Plan D, and call up her Plan B!

Many times women are very inconsistent in the signals they give out, which affects when or if a guy may initiate intimacy. They may want to portray themselves as a "*good* woman", and may over emphasize this so much that her date may feel uncomfortable making a move in an intimate way. Let me give you an example. Women often speak of being very religious and into their place of worship, and looking for a "spiritual, God-fearing man who puts God first." I'm going to step on some toes here, so I hope your stockings are thick! I've had a date (I'll call her Sarah) where we wound up having an ongoing discussion about her faith and activeness in it. For me, sex was not on my agenda considering this discussion! I did see some compromise in her position that she spoke of, and later, after the second or third date, she said I was "holding out and being stingy" regarding sex. While I do have spiritual values and some religiously based beliefs, at this time in my life I'm not living the life of a religious person. Yet the way I see it, if I was as righteous as she claimed she wanted her man to be, then I wouldn't be preparing for premarital sex, and I couldn't be with her at all. I would want a woman as determined to be abstinent as I am, and Sarah would call me Plan D because of having the spirituality she claimed she wanted in a man. If you're indecisive, then don't

131

proceed at all. And as my grandfather used to say, "Say what you mean, and mean what you say."

Remember ladies, men are not mind readers, and chemistry should be involved. If the vibe is cold and you're out of sync, don't be surprised if nothing develops.

Chapter 11:

Needs and Wants

Chapter 11: Needs and Wants

The Essential List

This is so crucial. If you don't know the difference between needs and wants, you'll have many unnecessary problems! You have to have clarity in yourself before you can get it from someone else. Otherwise, even if you get all you need from someone, you won't even realize what you have.

Write a list, and make a "needs" column and a "wants" column. Consider what's important to you, and ask yourself why. For example: Men, are you interested in a woman because you'd like to get to know her better to consider her as an S.O., or are you only interested in her sexually? Women, are you interested in a man's ability to handle his responsibilities and to know that he's progressive and working toward progressive goals, or are you concerned with what he has so you'll know what you can get, and how you'll be viewed by others by being with him? Financial means is something that most of us can learn. Yet, if someone doesn't have character, that takes longer to build, if the person is even striving for that goal at all.

Regarding needs and wants, write the needs first—the "I can't do without" items. The list should be listed in order of priorities even among all needs and the same with the wants column. Keep in mind that if the highest priorities are at the top, then even if they are all needs, the bottom must be secondary to the top. If your priorities are not in order, then you increase the chance of missing out on one of your top priorities. In my needs list example, the A, B, and C beside the item along with the numbers 1-3 can be a way to prioritize the list.

Before Making The List...

Consider these things before making your list: Men, if large breasts are important to you, then pursue that. If a woman wants a man 5' 9" or taller, then she should go for that. If it would just be a plus and not a need, then don't stress it, put it on the Wants side. Yet, if you'll feel slighted later because you really like a feature that your potential companion doesn't have, then don't disappoint yourself, put it on the Needs side. Consider though, that defining your requirements to detailed specifics will limit your options considerably, so be realistic.

Try to think about your needs not only for the present, but what you'll need and want in a few years. It may change, so think of your situation now and how it may be later if you are, or will be, looking for a long term companion. You may not want children now, but if you'll want that later, you need to know if your partner wants children, if they're capable of that, and if you want them to be your spouse or the other parent of your child. It's also good to think of their health; what's it like? These are just a few things to consider for the long term.

Think of your goals. If you're business oriented, you want someone who can complement you in that. If

Chapter 11: Needs and Wants

you're conservative, do they squander money? What about religious, political, or social views? If fitness is a serious part of your lifestyle, do they do anything for their own fitness?

NEEDS		WANTS	
(NO COMPROMISING!!!)			
A1	unmarried / uncommitted	**A1**	capable in business
A1	mentally / psychologically stable	**A1**	compatible hobbies
A1	STD free	**A2**	attractive
A1	sexuality / orientation	**B2**	5'7" or taller
A1	compatible character	**B3**	likes to cook
A1	love children	**C1**	get along well w/ family
A1	good grooming / hygiene		
A2	good physical shape		
B3	compatible goals		

NOTE:
The list will vary with different people and typically men and women have different priorities with the same item.

After you've done your list, hold on to it. We're going to use it later in this chapter. We'll compare it with

Chapter 11: Needs and Wants

an upcoming screening chart simulation we will examine, but I want you to make your list first, before you review the simulation.

Let's Test Your Priorities!

What really makes someone an *eligible* bachelor or bachelorette? For those interested in marriage, what makes you or your prospect good marriage material? If you could craft the perfect mate, based on your priorities, what would they be like? Let's do a simulation, using the population in a metropolitan city. To do this exercise, instead of listing all the things we want, we'll take the population totals and start taking away what we don't want. It's like taking a block of clay and carving off the excess to leave our masterpiece.

PLEASE NOTE: *This is a simulation, and not in any way exact. This is not a science book! This is only for the purpose of initiating and encouraging new thoughts and conversation, and to assist in re-evaluating priorities. Estimates are taken from sources such as the census bureau and other organizations, which in some cases do not specify the categories that I address. (See the appendix at the back of this book for reference sources). Some estimates have been taken from sheer guesswork, being as reasonable as possible based on relevant indications, implications and/or judgment. Some census bureau estimates were from 2004, and some were only available from 2000. I invite anyone who would like a specific breakdown of categories you're interested in, to* *gather the data for your area and use my blank data sheet, referred to below.*

First we'll look at data estimates on heterosexual females and then we'll look at heterosexual males. I have included a blank data sheet after the examples listed so you can obtain the stats for your local area if you'd like and work the numbers as it applies to your local area. Using the needs and wants list you created as a guide, you can apply your own list in a certain racial group, or you can add the numbers of more than one group and start subtracting from the total. This exercise is only a simulation, and yours will be very specific to your priorities. Admittedly, the age span is very wide but I wanted to include as many as possible in the dating scene. You'll need to consider ages within the age frame you're interested in. Needless to say, it will reduce your options greatly. We'll start with a population number, and just as you deduct funds from your bank account per transaction, we'll subtract and show the population balance as we screen out the factors not being sought after.

As our example, let's take Atlanta, Georgia. The metro area has an estimated population of 3,217,130. I include Fulton, Dekalb, Gwinnett, Clayton, Douglas, and Cobb counties.

Chapter 11: Needs and Wants

Estimated Metro Atlanta, Ga. Population -- 3,217,130

Heterosexual Females -- Options Available for Heterosexual Men

Note: This is by no means exact. Estimates are taken from averages From the following counties: Clayton, Cobb, DeKalb, Douglas, Fulton and Gwinnett. Number totals are rounded off (no fractions).

3,217,130 x 55% Female = 1,769,422

Screen OUT:	Black	White	Latina	Other
	35% = 619,298	57% = 1,008,570	7% = 123,859	1% = 17,694
All ages except 20-54	49% / 303,456	49% / 494,199	49% / 60,691	49% / 8,670
	315,842	514,371	63,168	9,024
Married	48% / 151,604	53% / 272,617	51% / 32,216	51% / 4,602
	164,238	241,754	30,952	4,422
Lesbian / Bi-sexual / trans	30% / 49,271	33% / 79,779	21% / 6,500	19% / 840
	114,967	161,975	24,452	3,582
STD+ Non curable medically	77% / 88,525	70% / 113,383	65% / 15,894	43% / 1,540
	26,442	48,592	8,558	2,042

Plan B, C, & D
The Men Women Choose When They Don't Have What They *Really* Want!

Screen OUT:	Black	White	Latina	Other
	26,442	48,592	8,558	2,042
Dangerously Mentally / psycol ill / subst abuse	11% / 2,909	12% / 5,831	8% / 685	6% / 123
	23,533	42,761	7,873	1,919
County Jail Inmates	10% / 2,353	3% / 1,283	7% / 511	1% / 19
	21,180	41,478	7,362	1,900
Poverty / below poverty	17% / 3,601	8% / 3,318	15% / 1,104	10% / 190
	17,579	38,160	6,258	1,710
Committed (truly)	15% / 2,637	18% / 6,869	20% / 1,252	18% / 308
	14,942	31,291	5,006	1,402

Chapter 11: Needs and Wants

Estimated Metro Atlanta, Ga. Population -- 3,217,130

Heterosexual Males -- Options Available for Heterosexual Females

Note: This is by no means exact. Estimates are taken from averages from the following counties:

Clayton, Cobb, DeKalb, Douglas, Fulton and Gwinnett. Number totals are rounded off (no fractions).

3,217,130 x 45% Male = 1,447,709

Screen OUT:	Black	White	Latino	Other
	35% = 506,698	57% = 825,194	7% = 101,340	1% = 14,477
All ages except 20-54	49% / 248,282	49% / 404,345	49% / 49,657	49% / 7,093
	258,416	**420,849**	**51,683**	**7,384**
Married	52% / 134,376	55% / 231,467	52% / 26,875	51% / 3,766
	124,040	**189,382**	**24,808**	**3,618**
Gay / Bi-sexual / trans	36% / 44,654	42% / 79,540	25% / 6,202	22% / 796
	79,386	**109,842**	**18,606**	**2,822**
STD+ Non curable medically	75% / 59,540	71% / 77,988	65% / 12,094	46% / 1,298
	19,846	**31,854**	**6,512**	**1,524**

Plan B, C, & D
The Men Women Choose When They Don't Have What They *Really* Want!

Screen OUT	Black	White	Latino	Other
	19,846	31,854	6,512	1,524
Dangerously Mentally / psycol ill / subst abuser	16% / 3,175	15% / 4,778	14% / 912	12% / 183
	16,671	27,076	5,600	1,341
County Jail Inmates	14% / 2,334	5% / 1,354	11% / 616	3% / 40
	14,337	25,722	4,984	1,301
Poverty / below poverty	16% / 2,294	6% / 1,543	12% / 598	8% / 104
	12,043	24,179	4,386	1,197
Committed (truly)	16% / 1,927	19% / 4,594	23% / 1,009	20% / 239
	10,116	19,585	3,377	958

Chapter 11: Needs and Wants

Estimated (city) _____ **Population --** _____

_____ **(gender) -- Options Available for** _____

  Note: Estimates are taken from averages from the following

counties: _____

Number totals are rounded off (no fractions).

Screen OUT:				

Plan B, C, & D
The Men Women Choose When They Don't Have What They *Really* Want!

Screen OUT:				

Chapter 11: Needs and Wants

Challenging Truths—Fewer Options: These figures don't even account for details such as:

- Both sexes want candidates to have a certain level of attraction; there's no way of knowing how many that would exclude with each person's personal taste.
- Ages 20-54? That age gap is HUGE. As you narrow down the ages to the range you specifically want, it reduces your options considerably.
- Many women want a tall man (6' and up). The average man in this country is 5'9" (certain geographical regions differ in averages).
- Some men want a tall woman, and the average woman in this country is 5'4" (some regions may vary).
- How compatible are your personalities?
- Compatible religion / spirituality?
- A person who can't / won't commit (if commitment is what you want)
- Is education compatibility an issue?
- Some want a specific hair texture or length
- Some want a specific skin complexion or eye color
- Are cultural or background differences an issue?
- Is the family or associates of the prospect an issue?
- For those who are overly sarcastic, arrogant (ego-itis), or have other unpleasant social skills, they reduce their options.
- Some people want someone who has no children or less than they may already have. (Ironically, a

parent can usually show what type of person they are in more ways and the kind of parent your possible future children will have by their current parent / child relationship).

- For men who don't mind bisexual women, the options are higher than the heterosexual female number listed; this dilutes the number of options for heterosexual women.
- Many (especially Sue) are interested in the financial means of a dating candidate—less than 50% of the Metro Atlanta population earn $50K or more (likely less than 40%) and many of them are married, your same gender, or have other exclusions. Needless to say, to find those who earn $100K or more, and who have discretionary funds (not overly consumed in debt) and are single and available; the options are few.
- Do you think my numbers for the STD+ factor was too high? Actually, I tried to lean to the conservative side on all of my figures. When you get to the chapter "Sex Sobriety", read carefully.

How many candidates does that leave? After considering the number of options you have available, along with others who may be interested in the same prospects as you, keep in mind that *your prospects have to be looking for someone like you!*

More Options:

- There are more people in Metro Atlanta than the census shows, because not only is it not this year's numbers but Atlanta has high transient

Chapter 11: Needs and Wants

traffic from other counties, as well as other cities.

- A number of residents are not documented
- While a positive STD status is unfortunate, some who are positive (and those that aren't) who choose to date others with a positive status have that option.
- I did not account for people married but separated. Some are moving towards divorce and therefore will become an available option.
- Some people date out of town, which reduces "competition" (for lack of a better word) for that gender.
- Some county jail inmates are released after a short term, and some state prisoners (which were not included) will be released and move back into Metro Atlanta. Some will pursue productive lives.

Take the needs list that you made earlier, and let's compare it with the screening chart. You can use Atlanta as your chart example like I did, and / or you can obtain the data for your city, and compare your list with your local screening chart data. The items you do want from your needs list, have to come from what's left from the screening chart (which omitted items you don't want). Ponder on that for a while, considering the "Challenging Truths—Fewer Options" and "More Options". Talk with a well adjusted and mature minded person (ideally someone who knows you fairly well) about your options from the chart, and ask their opinion regarding how realistic your list is, for a second opinion. As you confirm what your real needs are, it's important that you DON'T SETTLE. Unless of course, you re-examine the list and find it's not practical. You may very well do just that considering the list and the screening chart information. If you do change your needs list priorities, notice how much your thinking was altered. If so, I want you to rewrite another needs list, and compare the two. Also, I'd love to hear about the differences between the first and second list. Please send me an e-mail at my website.

Things Can Improve!

A friend asked me, "What if someone has their priorities in order and they're still single?" That is the case with a number of women. This is not intended to be pessimistic or dispiriting for them, though admittedly it could be. Keep being the wonderful person that you are, and as you continue to keep mindful and prayerful of what you have to offer someone, be aware ladies, that there is a sharpening of men taking place. While it's easy to have a negative view of the state of relationships and some men's disenchantment with commitment, there are also more books, radio shows and panel discussions on relationships than ever before, which men are getting more involved in. All forums where dialog on relationships is taking place, contributes to the critical need of communication between the sexes. I also believe that ladies are hearing more than ever the needs of men. Even when we don't agree, the dialog alone adds to understanding, and for those who listen, it benefits them. Not only that, but there are more single's groups and websites than ever. Let's dialog about our concerns, and then welcome avenues for mature people to interact.

Chapter 11: Needs and Wants

The Better Your List, The Better Your Results

Some people speak of seeking their soul mate. While I don't believe there's only one person living who could be considered a good soul mate for someone, depending on how realistic a person's expectations or priority list is, there may be fifty, three, or *no* people who fit the bill. Undoubtedly, you want the best for yourself. Just be clear about what constitutes "the best", and what's involved. Many of us have had such a lofty idea of the ideal mate and the details of how they should look and be; that for them to present themselves in that manner, in the right place, and the timing happen to be good for them and you in your life, AND for you to be just what THEY want, that would be a true act of God! Can it and has it happened? Sure it has. So pray for what you need and want, just keep in mind that we need to keep a reasonable perspective on things. Don't sacrifice the needs for the wants, and make sure the needs make sense. Some people (women and men both) turn away good options and then wonder why they're single or have to wind up settling for what's left from available options. Ladies, if you have your list in order and a hard working blue collar guy wants to talk to you but he's not the Lexis or BMW kind of guy, or doesn't wear the finest shoes, think twice before you turn him away. Guys, if your list is in order and you find a woman that you vibe with yet she has a few pounds more than you pictured or doesn't look quite like Eve from Eden, don't disregard the opportunity to see what's beyond the surface. I'm not saying take anything, but don't forget to look for character. If you can find everything in one package, then great. Yet that's very rare, so arrive early and take a number. By keeping firm to a *reasonable* needs / wants list, it can help you to not settle and yet get more of the things that are important to you.

Again, even with the final numbers listed on the screening charts, some of those people could live across town from you and have a totally different schedule. So how will you ever meet? Look for my network of social events in a city near you (as discussed in The 4 Level Dialog).

Chapter 11: Needs and Wants

FIXED

Constantly I hear the cry, 'A shortage of good men';
And while this statement does have truth, let's look at it again
What's good for one may not be what another searches for;
The expectations of each one, determines how we score
In my view, some ladies see what they've been groomed to
see;
Society, even their past, gives them their view of me
So many guys, just like me, who'd treat a lady right;
Miss the picture in their head, no option in their sight
There are needs that you <u>should</u> fill, no compromise in that;
But some are fixed on shallow things, and this is why they lack
Fixed on a man with pockets deep, one that's hard, thuggish;
They don't appreciate the rest, until they get their wish
But sometimes though, its how they're fixed, they don't mind
the abuse;
A guy with cash, can put them last, cause they just serve a use
Some are fixed as 'players', who will charm and thrill you too;
You can be a lady's prize, but one man just won't do
And for thug love, the risk is cool, that you could kiss his hand;
Cause for someone to treat you good, you don't respect that
man
Maybe it's the curse of Eve, or groomed by Satan's tricks;
But think of this when you complain—could it be, you've been
fixed?

NLC

Chapter 12:

Sex

Chapter 12:
Sex

Chemistry and Communication

Sex is such a serious thing in any kind of relationship that it, along with choices associated with it, can change your life forever. Of course, there's always the casual, just for fun factor in many people's lives. Even then when people don't attach the emotional significance to sex, it's still serious based on the dangers and responsibilities involved. As for now, let's discuss some things that could help to improve your sexual experience. This is not an all inclusive how-to chapter on sex, so we won't cover some topics such as sexual positions. We will, though, discuss some things that I feel may be useful to you.

First, as discussed earlier, you want to know that you and the person you are sexual with have a good vibe level. If not, the progression towards sex and even the act itself can be awkward. Some men and women alike are mutually interested only in casual sex, but often women look for a little more of a comfort level in who she's dealing with. Some men may be physically ready just knowing that there's a willing woman in front of them while others need to have more than that and be into the woman as a person to some degree.

Make an opportunity to talk about sex before you

engage in it. By doing this, you can get to know some of your partner's likes and dislikes and discuss yours also. If the other person is not very open in this discussion, they probably won't be comfortable with sex at this point. One reason that this discussion is critical is because y*ou must express what you don't do, just as (if not more) importantly as what you like to do.* Now for those of you that have no rules and anything goes, then I guess this doesn't apply to you! But for the rest of us, you must express yourself in this regard. Passion is very powerful, so if you don't draw your line, you could easily find yourself doing those very things. If you don't practice oral or anal sex for example, this is a good time to express that, and if your prospective partner is fixed on it, then they can decide if they're still interested in you; and you can decide if you're still interested in them. You don't want someone trying to spring a surprise on you, have to stop them and kill the mood, or even worse—compromise your stand. It's better they know where they can and can't go up front. Once you've predetermined what you are *not* willing to do, such as go without a condom, you **should not** compromise that. If you do, you could have great regrets later. When you compromise your stand for someone on something meaningful—whether it's by another person's persuasion or not—you often find that the other person has a small significance in your life anyway and it wasn't worth the compromise. Don't be afraid to stop the entire experience if your partner does not respect your stand. Also don't be afraid to stop the show if you see or feel something that makes you concerned in some way, whether physically in foreplay or psychologically.

Chapter 12: Sex

That being said, sometimes people can start the foreplay process and decide to stop the progression because they had never fully made up their mind about their decision to have sex before getting started. This can cause much unnecessary frustration. It's one thing to stop because something seemed to be off with the vibe and something different if it's based on indecisiveness. *If you're indecisive, it's better not to even get started!* For the record, if someone is trying to get together late at night or talking in a sexual nature, don't be naive about what they want to happen or take it as "just flirtation." If you're not ready for sex at this time, let them know up front. Also, if you invite someone into your home or go to his / hers past a certain time, it can give the impression that you're prepared and willing to have sex. While this may sound like an elementary statement to men, it's remarkable that so many women are surprised when they learn the guy seemed confident in his expectations, which she may say she never entertained the idea. This misunderstanding has at times contributed to very unpleasant experiences for some, especially where one of the parties may not be well adjusted psychologically. (You know, CRAZY!)

Plan B, C, & D
The Men Women Choose When They Don't Have What They *Really* Want!

Prior To Sex!

Some people choose to go to a doctor or testing facility together* and get tested for STD's before having sex, and they agree to stay monogamous. This is a *wonderful* thing. For those who do this with a view of having a relationship, we'll call this D.T.R. (Date-Test-Relationship). First, you date to determine if you're compatible enough to pursue a relationship and if so, you get tested together and go from there. Hopefully you have the chemistry to make things work. If not, at least you have more peace of mind that while you were together you knew what you were dealing with (generally speaking). Keep in mind though, there are incubation periods where a test may be negative (showing no disease) but an infection may be in the person's system. This is why testing should be repeated again no sooner than three months later, and be repeated for an ongoing period afterwards.

For those who choose to date and get tested with only an exclusive sexual arrangement in mind, we'll call that D.T.A. (Date-Test-Arrangement). Maybe you don't feel you have what it takes for a long-term relationship and choose the D.T.A. route. While having a D.T.A. for

*(This way, results of each can be seen, shared, and openly discussed with medical staff. Not only can they answer your questions, but it verifies the results are authentic and not typed up fictitiously.)

Chapter 12: Sex

health reasons is an understandable decision, it can become complicated. Typically in this arrangement, though you have agreed to be exclusive sexually, since you're not in an "official" relationship it's more likely that either party will call the agreement quits with little or no notice. The same can be true in a committed relationship, but since the D.T.A. lacks a level of commitment, it's generally more fragile and unpredictable. One challenge is that often, one will develop deeper feelings than the other person. Also, consideration should always be given to the possibility that the person you have sex with could become a parent to your child in an unplanned pregnancy. How much do you know about what type of parent he or she would make? I knew someone who had sex with a woman he didn't know. She became pregnant, and they tried to make a relationship work for a brief minute. They broke it off, she made it hard for him to see his daughter, and they began to hate one another. Considering how easily that can happen and how that affects all three of their lives, it's something to consider in our priorities.

Some may start with a D.T.A. and move into a relationship. Your views, needs and wants, and expectations in these matters should be discussed extensively up front when dating.

Interaction

Here's something I believe many women think and we men allow ourselves to be victims of this erroneous thinking: Many women act as though we should be the _one_ that makes the sexual experience good. Many of those that think that way probably do 25%

or less of the physical exertion. Then they hand out a "test paper" with a grade on it to let the guy know, not just how well he performed, but how good he IS. It's as if his actual worth in the present and future is determined by her. Sex does involve a measure of skill to make it a more enjoyable experience, but being good also involves a level of chemistry between the two. Remember: "It takes two to tango!" Women, you could be naked and willing but you still have to put in work to make it a more pleasurable experience for the man too! It really does make a difference, ladies; because here's something you may or may not know: Men can have sex and even ejaculate without having had a full erection. The level of a man's stimulation affects the extent of the erection. The "size matters" issue is nothing new, so if a woman isn't understanding his needs and serving them in addition to getting served herself, then she's not doing her part to get his full potential in size and / or firmness.

Don't just be present during the action, but participate. Here again, if what pleases him is something you don't want to do, then you should've gotten to know that from the pre-sex dialog and not been in this situation. Likewise, if you just don't know what works for your partner, then conversation ahead of time perhaps *could* have prevented a stale experience if the rest of your chemistry is good. Keep in mind; talking about sex doesn't have to kill spontaneity, but can even be used to mentally arouse each other in a flirtatious manner. Keep it fun. For the ladies, we'll cover some of the things that we men like in foreplay. Also for the guys, we'll cover a little about foreplay with women and things that may help guys last longer during the act of intercourse. This will be a work in progress; a practice, and not a "flip the switch

Chapter 12: Sex

and see results" kind of thing.

First, let's address the psychology behind some expressions relating to sex. This may bring some debate from the ladies. Sex is a giving act, in that you are sharing something with the other person that's very deep and personal. Even if a person doesn't attach that type of meaning to sex, if nothing else it's deep due to the interaction and even the possible responsibilities or dangers that can come with it. It's also giving in the time aspect. Aside from that, let's discuss the giving factor. It's commonly said that women "give" men sex, or P****. Men are therefore often seeking to "receive" as often as possible. He feels he's enriching himself somehow, by "getting" all he can.

"Can I have some...?" There's a psychology that comes with this. The giver always has the upper hand, being able to deny or cut off the recipient at any time. The giver has the power. Women have always had a power over men. Their ability to get what they want from a man can be endless if they understand him. (Try not to abuse this, ladies...ok?) While there is nothing that can substitute what a woman can offer, we should understand something that could help us to have a more balanced view. Who is really giving to whom? In sex, the woman may be open, but she is waiting to *receive* what a man has to give. She takes in, the man puts out. Even in the case of semen, whether a condom is used or not; he is giving out, and she receives. She gets moist or wet, but isn't pouring into the man; He is pouring into her. In the physical exertion also, the man is usually doing most of the work of giving. In actuality, men are hoping to find a willing recipient of what *he* has to *give*. He just may not think of it in that way. Men, if a woman doesn't want what you have to give, you may need to think of it differently than you have in the past. Don't feel that you've failed or that you have to *take* what she wouldn't give, to show your strength. If she doesn't want it, there's someone else who will. Considering the seriousness of sex and even the power of possible procreation when climaxing, men should be careful and selective of when and to whom they give themselves to anyway. Of course this is easier said than done, but beneficial. Again, words can't describe my appreciation for women. *No one or nothing can take your place!* Still, we have to see it in the proper perspective. Know your worth as a man. It will boost the self-esteem of those men who need it and help to empower the mind and spirit. Women have known the power of their influence (and body) since the beginning of time.

What He Likes

Regarding some of the things that men like, details will vary with the person. Generally speaking, men are very visual. We like to get into you ladies visually first, as a form of foreplay. When the time comes for it, wear something revealing or sexy. If you're out in public he may want you to dress revealingly sexy and enjoy the way it makes him look (a stroke for his ego); or he may be the type that prefers to see your suggestive attire in a private setting. Regarding foreplay, either change into something sexy or at least have on sexy underwear. It makes a difference. Give him an exotic dance and entice him. You don't have to do a full song dance, but don't be afraid to do seductive things like this. It's always a plus. It'll help him get ready mentally and

Chapter 12: Sex

physically. Pose for him. Tease him.

Ladies, hear me on this. Women have multiple sexual organs or regions. Even if a guy isn't the most proficient at doing it, likely he'll generally give attention to each part on a woman. Men only have one sexual organ below the neck (in a heterosexual relationship), and many women will only handle it when they're preparing for insertion (if at all). Though women typically like to be fondled in foreplay, they may be slow about stimulating their partner in this way. Learn to stimulate your partner in foreplay. Just remember, before the climax we don't produce as much moisture as you ladies do, so it helps if your hands (or, whatever) aren't dry! A petroleum based lubricant such as Vaseline has the best feel for someone in a committed relationship who has chosen not to use a condom. If that's not the case, be sure to use a lubricant that won't break down or weaken the condom such as Vagisil or KY. (Caution: This form of foreplay has a risk if you don't know the STD status of your partner is negative. This is best experienced with a monogamous partner who is STD free.)

During sex, some men like to be the aggressor, and some like the woman to be. I've talked to women that said their S.O. (significant other) won't initiate sex or seem to want her to do most of the work. Communication is definitely needed to express your needs and wants in this regard. Make sure he is open and honest with you on this because it could be that he is not very emotionally involved due to apathy (his or yours), or your chemistry may not be blending. This could also be due to unresolved issues in your relationship, whether you are aware of the issues or not.

Some men like a woman to be "freaky" and do

various erotic things, and for some that may be a turn off. It's important to know what works for your partner. Everyone has their preferences and expectations, but again it's necessary to know if there is a "line" drawn and where it is.

As far as stimulating your partner and improving sex, read material like *The One Hour Orgasm—How To Learn The Amazing Venus Butterfly Technique* by Drs. Robert and Leah Schwartz, PhD. It speaks of open communication and ways to stimulate your partner intensely, among other helpful information. It may also be helpful to read some information on Kama Sutra lovemaking techniques.

The Power of The...

Some women practice Kegel exercises. They are contractions that Dr. Arnold Kegel made popular starting in or around 1948, but have been practiced by different cultures for many years. It was designed to be a non-surgical remedy to help incontinence and uterine prolapse in women (the loss of control over urine leakage and loss of elasticity in the vagina). This is sometimes an issue with age. Also, after childbirth a woman's vagina may take some time to get back to its previous size or feel. At times her partner may complain that sex doesn't feel as good, and even lose interest in sex with that partner. One man I interviewed said he couldn't even feel his partner's insides, not the bottom (uterus), or any walls at all. It affected his self-esteem.

Many women speak of a man's penis size being very important. Especially for women in a relationship, if this is an issue, you should practice these contractions.

Chapter 12: Sex

They can help to tighten the vagina, and even if your partner is small, you'll be smaller so the fit will be better. The contractions involve the pubococcygeus muscles, which are the muscles used if you stop yourself from urinating. As with any exercise, you may need to consult your doctor first. (I had to put that in there!) There are methods such as contracting the muscles and letting go, and repeating it for 5 to 10 times, three times a day; and other methods. You can go online to read more about it or purchase books on the subject. With practice over time, some women have reported being able to put pressure on a single finger inserted in the vagina when she contracts these muscles.

In my opinion, a woman should practice this in moderation. If she is too small, it can be uncomfortable and / or hinder his erection. Or, it could be so 'fitted' on the penis that it could produce a premature ejaculation. In this case it could feel great (to the guy), but obviously the result is unwanted. While some complain about a loose fit, if she's not too tight it can actually make sex last longer. If Kegel exercises are practiced in balance, a woman can contract her vagina at will during intercourse, and produce incredible sensations for her partner and herself. The contractions can stimulate the clitoris and enhance her orgasms, and provide intense pulling sensations for him when done with the right timing and rhythm. I've even heard of a woman who, when straddling her partner with him inside of her, could make him produce a climax without moving her body; but by only using Kegel contractions!

What She Likes

Stimulating a woman in foreplay usually starts with a psychological attraction, which contributes to setting the mood. Once it becomes physical, it's (usually) best to have a gradual progression towards her intense places, and the more intense activities. As you progress, caressing her vaginal area can be very stimulating; but start slow, from the outside. If she doesn't resist your going inside, you'll find her G-spot is at the upper (inner) wall, as if you put your finger straight in and motioned your finger to say, "come here." While this is a sensitive area, it's not an automatic "trigger" but produces the most sensation after she has been stimulated for a period of time. Basically, don't neglect the north, south, east or west walls! (Especially the north and south walls.) Remember, each woman is individual so they may really enjoy this foreplay, or may not be as into it as others. Talk to your partner to see what works best for her; and if / when you do this, verify you're not applying too much pressure. Also, make sure she's not dry when you do this, otherwise instead of stimulation, it'll be abuse! (Caution: This form of foreplay has a risk if you don't know the STD status of your partner is negative. This is best experienced with a monogamous partner who is STD free.)

As an artist would rarely paint the same picture repeatedly, sex is individual for each experience, and should not be redundant. If you're with the same partner for some time, remember to keep it fresh and creative. Keep in mind different places, positions, tempos, settings, and situations that will keep it lively. Women usually enjoy receiving oral sex, but I have interviewed some

Chapter 12: Sex

who said their partner did a poor job of stimulating her in this way. In that case, they usually prefer him not to even bother. (Be sure your hygiene is impeccable!) Communication in sex is vital for the best experience, yet if a partner doesn't know even the basics of a woman's body, then it will detract from the mood. Again, Dr. Schwartz' book should help with this. One major concern for women in sex, is her partner's ability to make it last.

Make It Last!

It's a well-established fact that women don't want a "minute man." As far as making sex endure, there are many factors that affect the experience. I have had endurance that we were both very pleased with (encore recipient!), and experiences where I, let's say, failed to deliver. I've had a partner who, if she talked to another partner of mine about our experience, they would think they were talking about two different people! I have though, learned of things that help in the consistency of longer lasting sex. First, there's no question that sex is really very mental. Guys, if you're very excited and you're overwhelmed by having this woman, then you won't last. Even if she's a 10, you have to think of it as no big deal. This may be hard to do, but it's necessary. Think of her as just another average female. Or maybe it's the opposite. If she's not so exciting, you may have to think of stimulating thoughts if you're having erection issues. Still, as mentioned earlier, the best thing is to have someone you blend with. Good chemistry is better and more natural than using psychological tricks. Regarding impotence, it could be due to a number of things, such as: stress, anxiousness, fear, fatigue, a previous climax that was too recent, a disturbed conscience, or any number of mental or psychological issues causing unrest. It could also be physical issues so a visit to the urologist may be helpful if it's a continual problem.

Also, the man's potency and endurance can be affected by the woman he's with. No, this is not a blame shifting thing. If she hasn't had sex in some time, just as discussed earlier about over doing Kegel exercises, her vagina may feel like a closed fist! Again, it can produce a premature ejaculation. This tight fit may especially be the case for a woman who has not had children. Some women masturbate in ways that keeps their vagina loose (such as with certain sex toys). Each woman has to decide what's best for her, but she should be aware that her fit can definitely affect the endurance of sex. Her partner using his fingers in foreplay as described earlier can help to loosen her to some degree. If she and her partner have sex again in a short period of time (maybe a day or so) he may start to feel a difference. If they go too long before having sex again, they may be back at square one! It may help to discuss it openly and make plans to work on it in a short term, consecutive manner. In a case like this, ladies, patience is required if you want a successful experience. This is one of the many advantages to monogamy. Consistent sex in a monogamous relationship can be the best sex there is!

Often, early in intercourse there is a sensitive period that a man has to get through. If we're successful getting through that without an ejaculation, we can have a good endurance experience. If it has been a while since a man has had sex, then he may be more of a sprinter. He should determine when it's a good time for his body.

Chapter 12: Sex

If he has had a climax one to three days (the time may vary) before he's ready for the marathon, this may help. This is not an exact science though. In fact it *could* be just the opposite. At times having climaxed recently could make him more sensitive. It's basically keeping the penis familiar with the sensation, which could make it easy to happen again. If it's been a while it may need to work longer before it remembers what a climax feels like. I think this is more of the "moody penis" exception, however, and not the rule. Each person should learn his own body to know if it's usually one way or the other for him.

Like women, men can also strengthen their pubococcygeus muscles, which can help prevent premature ejaculation. Again guys, this can be done by tightening your muscles as if you're trying to stop yourself from urinating. You can do this ten times and on the tenth time hold it for five seconds. Try this two to three times per day. This is not an over night fix, but with practice it can make a difference. If you tighten these muscles during intercourse to prevent a climax and you wait too long and get too close to the ejaculation, the contraction could *induce* the climax instead of holding it back. Lastly, use good judgment. If you feel you're going to climax before you're ready, slow down or stop. Wait a few minutes if you have to. I'm sure your partner would rather that than to end the whole experience too soon. Learn your body and its limits, and when you'll need to stop before you climax. It may be difficult to get control when you feel very close to a climax, even when you try to pace yourself. It is important to get started at a good time for your body as described earlier. You may also need to reduce the amount of foreplay your partner performs on you, or change the type of foreplay.

Don't Fake It!

Now ladies, we do want you to be into the experience and "feeling" it, but some (perhaps many) women go so far as to fake orgasms. Why, when you only deprive yourself? In interviews I've heard women say, "It's to end it, 'cause I wasn't enjoying it." Again, that's one of the advantages in talking about sex first, so you can learn one another. There are some things that should be known as a given (unless you're dealing with a virgin who has received bad advice), but if you're going to get to that level of intimacy, then you might as well share the needed information about your likes and dislikes to make it a good experience. Whether it's to end it or to boost his ego, think how much better it would be to communicate and make the orgasms happen for real! If he's too proud to listen to you as if he knows it all, let him know that "It could be even better if..." If he doesn't make adjustments and you know you've made yourself clear on the *what* and the *how*, then maybe he's selfish and you're just not compatible sexually.

How Long Is Too Long?

Ok, here's something that tripped me out. I've had sex where I out lasted my partner, without ever climaxing or losing my, I'll say, "charge". With one partner it happened twice (the only times we had sex) and she felt frustrated and her pride was hurt, saying, "This has never happened to me before." I was very

Chapter 12: Sex

attracted to her and the experience was very enjoyable to me, as I was confident it was to her. Still, she asked, "What's wrong with me?" I tried to assure her that nothing was wrong with her, and I was very much into her and the experience, but she was unsettled. I said, "I thought that's what women wanted" [long duration sex— the longer the better]. There was nothing I could say to change how she felt at that time. I noticed that though she acted as if it was only circumstantial, through her actions she chose not to be intimate with me again. In fact, I haven't seen her in person since! Another female told me that she had the same experience with her partner. The sex lasted a long time, she enjoyed it, and had several orgasms yet she called it "A horrible experience." Why? "Because he never had a climax," she said. This gave her feelings of inadequacy and made her feel bad about herself. She also questioned if he was promiscuous, but the biggest issue she had was how it made her feel about herself. The truth is, if the guy isn't into it and enjoying it, he wouldn't be able to keep his erection, especially after going for a long time. I explained this to the female who told me her experience. Another female told me that some of her partners have told her that if their erection is too hard, it's difficult for them to have a climax. Here again, the experience is generally closely tied with the man's excitement with her (unless he has taken some type of drug or supplement which affects the erection). So if anything, she should view it as a compliment!

This is a small example to show how the "all night long sex" propaganda is just that: propaganda. Men hear about women's criticism of a man's duration, and while sometimes it may be valid, sexual compatibility is very achievable. We men sometimes buy into the view of women being insatiable, but women are not robots. By overcoming this overwhelming perception, it can help men to reduce feelings of intimidation that can lead to impotence and / or premature ejaculation. This supports the point of how consistency in a committed relationship allows communication, patience, self confidence, trust, and concern for the other person to help both people to get to their peak and produce the best possible experiences. This is not just the case in one sexual act, but in the relationship as a whole.

Chapter 12: Sex

10 Things That Can Help to Improve Sex

1. Your partner and you should have a good vibe—mental / psychological chemistry.

2. Communicate! Discuss needs, likes, dislikes, and things that are off limits. Don't assume this partner has the same preferences as the last.

3. Make sure you know your and your partner's STD/STI status! Get tested for safety and to reduce these distracting concerns.

4. I know all of my readers already do this, but just for the record; **KEEP IMPECCABLE HYGEINE!!!**

5. Read sex education material like *The One Hour Orgasm—How To Learn The Amazing Venus Butterfly Technique* by Drs. Robert and Leah Schwartz, Phd. and read about Kama Sutra techniques.

6. Consider your (and your partner's) biological timing. Men, make sure your last climax was not too recent, and not too long ago. Women, keep a good track of your cycle's calendar!

7. Foreplay is the first half of sex. It's in your flirting and courting before you ever touch one another, and in your chemistry. Also, be sure to give ample time to enjoy each other physically before

intercourse. Tease each other a little… but don't over do it!

8. **USE CONDOMS!!!** Regardless of test results, use condoms until you have mutually determined not to do so. Never under any circumstances have unprotected sex without adequate testing AND a commitment.

9. Do Kegel exercises—(Both men and women). Men: It helps your erection and endurance / control of ejaculation. Women: Kegel exercises help to tighten the vagina and gives greater sensation for men. Do it with balance so it's not too tight, but can be tightened at your will. It helps to stimulate the clitoris during sex and enhances orgasms. If he has a small penis, it is a must for you; he'll feel larger, have more confidence, and it enhances the sensation for you both. During intercourse, these contractions can give him the sensation that you're "jacking" his penis with your vagina.

10. Keep sex fresh and interesting, and be willing to change your environment and routine.

Chapter 13:

Sex Sobriety

Chapter 13:
Sex Sobriety

First of all, I am not a doctor or health professional and give no medical advice herein. For medical advice, see your healthcare professional.

Ok, this subject is critical, though I know some don't like to think about these things. I warn you now: This information will get deep, so if you're ready to be informed, brace yourself! Let's discuss some of the facts about STD transmission. Then we'll discuss safety decisions. Some data resources use the acronym STI instead of, or along with, STD. It stands for sexually transmitted infection.

You'd Know If You Had A Disease, Right?

The following is what the American Social Health Association says about the difference between an STD and an STI:

"Diseases that are spread through sexual contact are usually referred to as 'sexually transmitted diseases'—STDs for short. In recent years, however, many experts in this area of public health have suggested replacing STD with a new term: Sexually Transmitted Infection, or STI.

Why? The concept of 'disease', as in STD, implies a clear medical problem, usually some obvious signs or symptoms. But in truth several of the most common STDs have no signs or symptoms in the majority of persons infected. Or they have mild signs and symptoms that can be easily overlooked. So the sexually transmitted virus or bacteria can be described as creating 'infection', which may or may not result in 'disease.' This is true of Chlamydia, gonorrhea, herpes, and human papillomavirus (HPV), to name a few.

For this reason, in some of the published literature, the term 'disease' is being replaced by 'infection.' ASHA has used the term STD since 1988 and it appears in hundreds of published ASHA documents, including many of these web pages. Users of this website will continue to see it for some time.

Moving forward, however, you will also begin to see increased use of the term STI."

[End of ASHA data]

Most of the references in this book will use STD, since that is the most commonly used acronym by my resources. Here's a real paradox to the acronym STD and STI: Many people have gotten them (particularly HSV-1) and they weren't transmitted by sex, but by kissing. In rare cases passionate kissing can transmit HIV or Hepatitis, but more commonly HSV-1 (herpes type 1) can be transmitted from a simple, non-passionate lip kiss, if you kiss at an "active" time.

Chapter 13: Sex Sobriety

Acting On Knowledge Is Power; Fear Of It Is Dangerous

Please note: Even though some of this information is dreadful, there are treatments to make them more livable today than in the past. Please don't allow fear to prevent you from getting tested. Just as with cancer and any other illness, it is vital to your health to diagnose and treat an STD as early as possible. It is also vital to prevent the spread to others. Remember, there are people who know or suspect they have an STD, but will never tell you before having sex with you. I went out with a young lady once, and we corresponded for a short time afterwards. She inquired about spending the weekend with me on a couple of occasions. After my informing her about my requirement for STD testing before sex, she told me that she had a positive STD status. That's just a *small* example of the **power of acting on critical information!** I've also had someone just fade off of the scene before taking it further. For someone who does know they have a positive status and tells their partner or prospective partner before sex, what a respectable thing to do! If you're STD+ and ready for sex, give the other person the right to make the choice.

There are some diseases that are curable, yet dreadful if acquired. Not only that, but many are acquired by a condom not being used, which means a person has also exposed themselves to the risk of HIV / AIDS and everything else.

I won't spend a lot of time on statistics for the diseases that are curable, but I will say they can be dangerous, embarrassing, and challenging to get rid of. This doesn't mean that if something is not mentioned here that it is curable, but I'm only mentioning a few things that I feel is little known or understood. For a more extensive list of STD's and information on them, you may refer to the websites of the CDC, The American Social Health Association, WebMD, or a current encyclopedia. (See the Appendix at the back of this book). Also, talk to your healthcare professional. While there are cures for certain STD's, some diseases can scar and change the appearance of your genital area permanently. Not to mention syphilis. It is curable, but if not treated in time, here's some of what the American Social Health Association (ashastd.org) had to say about syphilis:

Syphilis

Late Stage (Tertiary)
Symptoms of late stage or tertiary syphilis can occur 2 to 30+ years after infection.
Complications during this stage can include: gummas (small bumps or tumors that can develop on the skin, bones, liver or any other organ), *problems with heart and blood vessels, or chronic nervous system disorders, such as blindness, insanity and paralysis.*
If treated during this period, gummas will usually disappear. Though treatment at this phase will cure the disease and stop future damage to the body, **it cannot repair or reverse the damage that occurred before treatment.**
Most of the reported syphilis cases are in the Southeast of the country, with a higher percentage of cases among African-Americans than whites. In 2001, the South had the highest rate of syphilis, accounting for 56% of reported cases in the US.

Chapter 13: Sex Sobriety

The following discusses Hepatitis:

What is hepatitis?
Hepatitis is an inflammation of the liver that can be caused by a group of viruses. There are five major types of viral hepatitis:

Hepatitis A (HAV)	Hepatitis B (HBV)	Hepatitis C (HCV)	Hepatitis D (HDV)	Hepatitis E (HEV)

HAV, HBV and HCV are the most common types of viral hepatitis found in the United States.

How does someone get hepatitis?
The hepatitis A virus can enter a person's body when he or she eats or drinks something contaminated with the stool or blood of someone who has the disease. Symptoms usually appear suddenly, but are not followed by the chronic (long-lasting) problems that hepatitis B and C viruses can cause. The hepatitis B virus can infect a person if his or her mucous membranes or blood are exposed to an infected person's blood, saliva, semen, or vaginal secretions. Hepatitis C is spread by contact with the blood of an infected person. Symptoms appear more gradually than in hepatitis A. Unlike hepatitis A, the hepatitis B and C viruses can stay in the body–sometimes for a lifetime–and eventually cause chronic, serious liver diseases.

Plan B, C, & D
The Men Women Choose When They Don't Have What They *Really* Want!

What are the symptoms of hepatitis?
When hepatitis viruses damage liver cells, scar tissue is formed and those cells can no longer function. With fewer healthy liver cells, the body begins to show symptoms ranging from mild (such as fatigue) to more severe symptoms (such as mental confusion).

What are the complications of hepatitis?
Although many cases of hepatitis are not a serious threat to health, the disease can sometimes become chronic (long-lasting) and may lead to liver failure and death. In many cases, though, viral hepatitis is a self-resolving illness.

Is hepatitis sexually transmitted?
Sexual activity poses a different level of risk for each type of viral hepatitis, but is most closely associated with HBV. Blood transfusion, IV needle sharing, and organ transplants may also pose a risk for transmission.

Is there a way to prevent infection with hepatitis?
Hepatitis A and B are preventable through vaccination, though no vaccination currently exists for hepatitis C or E. Since hepatitis D only infects persons with active hepatitis B, the vaccine for hepatitis B prevents hepatitis D. For more information, see specific HAV, HBV, HCV, HDV and HEV sections.
One out of 20 people in the United States will get infected with hepatitis B (HBV) some time during their lives. [10] Hepatitis B is 100 times more infectious than HIV. [11] Approximately half of HBV infections are transmitted sexually. [12] HBV is linked to chronic liver disease, including cirrhosis and liver cancer.

Chapter 13: Sex Sobriety

Hepatitis A and hepatitis B are the only two vaccine-preventable STDs.

[End of ASHA data—italics mine]

In my research to make this information useful to my readers, I found out about STDs that I had never even heard of before. We'll discuss that later. It's serious out there! The following was taken from the website of the Centers for Disease Control and Prevention (CDC) or the National Prevention Information Network (NPIN), a CDC organization.

Genital warts:

Genital warts are caused by human papillomavirus (HPV). HPV is the name of a group of viruses that includes about 100 different strains or types, and more than 30 are sexually transmitted. They can infect the genital area of men and women, the penis, vulva (outside of the vagina), the anus, cervix, or rectum. Many who have mild forms of HPV have no symptoms and are unaware they have it, but can transmit it to a sex partner. In more serious forms, HPV can lead to cancer of the cervix, vulva, vagina, penis, or anus. In rare occasions a mother giving vaginal birth can pass HPV to the child, with the child developing warts in the throat or the voice box.
Approximately 20 million people are infected with HPV. At least 50 percent of sexually active men and women will acquire HPV at some point in their lives. By age 50,

at least 80 percent of women will have acquired genital HPV infection. About 5.5 million Americans get a new HPV infection each year.

Genital warts may appear as soft, moist, pink or flesh colored swellings usually in the genital area. They may be raised or flat, one or multiple, large or small and are sometimes shaped like cauliflower. Infection is possible to go away on its own, but there is no cure for HPV infection.

[End of the CDC information. The following is from ASHA regarding HPV:]

- Genital HPV is spread through skin-to-skin contact, not through an exchange of bodily fluid. Genital HPV cannot be entirely prevented by condom use.

- This virus is often asymptomatic – people usually don't know they have it.

- About 5.5 million new genital HPV cases occur each year – this is about 1/3 of all new STD infections.

- About 20 million people – men and women – are thought to have an active HPV infection at any given time.

- Nearly three out of four Americans between the ages of 15 and 49 have been infected with genital HPV in their lifetime.

- HPV can be contracted from one partner, remain dormant, and then later be unknowingly

Chapter 13: Sex Sobriety

transmitted to another sexual partner, including a spouse.

- Though usually harmless, some types cause cervical cancer.

- About 14,000 cases of cervical cancer are diagnosed in the United States each year.

- Over 5,000 women each year die of cervical cancer in the United States.

How common is HPV?
HPV is the most common sexually transmitted virus. It has been estimated that 75% or more of sexually active Americans will contract HPV sometime in their lives. This means that *anyone* who has ever had sexual relations has a high chance of being exposed to this virus, but only a small number of women infected with HPV develop cell changes that need to be treated. In almost all cases, the immune system will keep the virus (including the cancer-related HPV types) under control or get rid of it completely. However, if HPV infection does not go away over many years, there is a greater chance of developing cell changes that may lead to cervical cancer. Only very rarely does the presence of HPV lead to cervical cancer.

Can HPV infections be treated?
There is currently no treatment available for the virus itself. However, good treatments do exist for the diseases HPV can cause, such as cervical cell changes or genital warts. Your healthcare

provider will discuss these treatment options with you, if you need them.

I am 30 or older – Should I get the HPV test in addition to my Pap test?

In women 30 and over, screening using both an HPV test and a Pap test is more likely to find abnormal cervical cell changes than either test alone. If both tests are negative (normal), a woman may safely have her next Pap and HPV test in three years depending on her past Pap test findings and other risk factors. For this reason, some women now may have an HPV test when they have their Pap test. It will still be important to continue having routine recommended preventative health exams.

I am under age 30 – Should I get the HPV test in addition to my Pap test?

Consensus guidelines do not currently recommend this. HPV is very common in women under the age of 30 and cervical cancer is very rare in this age group. Most women under 30 with HPV will get rid of the virus without treatment. So including an HPV test along with your Pap isn't helpful for younger women and might be harmful if it resulted in too many tests and unnecessary treatment. After age 30, HPV is much less common. If you are over the age of 30 and you test positive for HPV you may have gotten it many years before and your immune system hasn't gotten rid of it. Because HPV must be present for many years to cause cell changes, testing for HPV after the age of 30 is much more helpful.

Chapter 13: Sex Sobriety

If I tested positive for HPV, what does this mean for me?

Most HPV infections go away without treatment because the immune system finds the virus and either gets rid of it or suppresses it to the point that it is unlikely to cause additional problems. Cell changes that may eventually lead to cervical cancer only occur when this does not happen and HPV stays for many years. Even though HPV is found in cervical cancer, most people testing positive for HPV are not at risk for getting cervical cancer because they have the virus for only a short time (months rather than many years). Therefore, women with a normal Pap who test positive for HPV will usually be tested for HPV again in 6-12 months. Testing positive a second time does not mean that there is great risk of cervical cancer, or even of cell changes that may lead to cervical cancer, but it does mean that further evaluation will likely be recommended.

If I test positive for HPV, how did I get it?

HPV is usually acquired by direct skin-to-skin contact during intimate sexual contact with someone who is infected. Most men and women are not aware that they have the virus. Condoms do not offer complete protection from HPV. Increasing numbers of partners increases the risk of getting HPV, but the virus is so common that having only a single lifetime partner does not assure protection. It is usually impossible to determine when, and from whom, HPV was caught. HPV may be detected fairly soon after exposure, or may not be found until many years later. For all these reasons, it is not helpful, nor fair to blame your partner.

What does my positive HPV test mean for my partner?

Most sexually active couples share HPV until the immune response eliminates the infection. Partners who are sexually intimate only with each other are not likely to pass the same virus back and forth. When HPV infection goes away the immune system will remember that HPV type and keep a new infection of the same HPV type from occurring again. However, because there are many different types of HPV, becoming immune to one HPV type may not protect you from getting HPV again if exposed to another HPV type.

If I have HPV or a cell abnormality, is there anything I can do?

Don't smoke. Smoking has been shown to increase the chance that cell abnormalities might progress to more severe changes. Be sure to keep your follow-up doctor appointments.

Will I have the HPV virus forever?

Probably not. HPV infection is very common, but it usually clears, or is suppressed by the immune system, within 1-2 years.

[This marks the end of the ASHA information. The following is from the CDC website:]

Herpes:

Genital herpes is a sexually transmitted disease caused by herpes simplex virus type 1 and type 2 (HSV-1) and (HSV-2). Most people have minimal or no symptoms.

Chapter 13: Sex Sobriety

When symptoms do occur, they generally appear as blisters around the genital or rectal area. The blisters break, leaving soars that may take two to four weeks to heal the first time they occur. The outbreaks' length of time decreases over a period of years. There are treatments that may reduce the number of outbreaks, but there is no cure for herpes.

Nationwide, at least 45 million people age 12 and up, one out of five adolescents and adults, have had genital HSV infection. HSV-1 can cause genital herpes, but more commonly causes soars of the mouth and lips, so-called "fever blisters." HSV-1 can be caused by oral to genital contact or genital to genital contact with someone who has HSV-1.

HSV-1 and HSV-2 can be transmitted from the soars the viruses cause, but can also be transmitted between outbreaks from skin that does not appear to be broken and does not appear to have a soar. A person almost always gets HSV-2 infection during sexual contact with someone who has a genital HSV-2 infection but may not know that they are infected and may not have a visible sore.

Most people infected with HSV-2 are not aware of their infection. However, if signs and symptoms occur during the first outbreak, they can be quite pronounced. The first outbreak usually occurs within two weeks after the virus is transmitted, and the sores typically heal within two to four weeks. Other signs and symptoms during the primary episode may include a second crop of sores, and flu-like symptoms, including fever and swollen glands. However, most individuals with HSV-2 infection may never have sores, or they may have very mild signs that they do not even notice or that they mistake for insect bites or another skin condition.

Most people diagnosed with a first episode of genital herpes can expect to have several outbreaks (symptomatic recurrences) a year (typically four or five). Over time these recurrences usually decrease in frequency.

In addition, genital HSV can cause potentially fatal infections in babies if the mother has sores at the time of delivery. It is important that women avoid contracting herpes during pregnancy because a first episode during pregnancy causes a greater risk of transmission to the baby. If a woman has active genital herpes at delivery, a cesarean delivery is usually performed. Fortunately, infection of a baby from a woman with herpes infection is rare.

Worldwide, herpes may play a role in the heterosexual spread of HIV, the virus that causes AIDS. Herpes can make people more susceptible to HIV infection, and it can make HIV-infected individuals more infectious.

__Genital ulcer diseases can occur in both male and female genital areas that are covered or protected by a latex condom,__ as well as in areas that are not covered. Correct and consistent use of latex condoms can *reduce* the risk of genital herpes *only when the infected area or site of potential exposure is protected. Since a condom may not cover all infected areas, even correct and consistent use of latex condoms cannot guarantee protection from genital herpes.*

Persons with herpes should abstain from sexual activity with uninfected partners when lesions or other symptoms of herpes are present. *It is important to know that even if you do not have any symptoms you can still infect your*

Chapter 13: Sex Sobriety

sex partner. Even if there are no symptoms, sex partners of infected persons should be advised that they may become infected.

[End of CDC content—the following is some of the information from ASHA on herpes:]

1. About 50 to 80 percent of American adults have oral herpes, which is commonly called cold sores or fever blisters.

2. *About one in four* adults in the United States has genital herpes. However, most people don't know they are infected because their symptoms are too mild to notice or mistaken for another condition.

3. With more than 50 million adults in the US with genital herpes and up to 1.6 million new infections each year, some estimates suggest that by 2025 up to 40% of all men and half of all women could be infected. [14,15,16]

4. Herpes is most easily spread from genital-to-genital or oral-to-genital contact during an active outbreak or during prodrome – the few days just before an outbreak.

5. Oral and genital herpes can be uncomfortable, but they are generally not dangerous infections in healthy adults.

6. Herpes does not affect the immune system. It is rare for adults to have any health problems from genital herpes.

7. However, having genital herpes makes it easier to acquire and/or transmit HIV, a virus that can cause AIDS.

8. There are several days throughout the year when herpes can be spread even when no symptoms are present (called asymptomatic reactivation or asymptomatic shedding).

9. Suppressive (daily) antiviral therapy with valacyclovir has also been proven to reduce the risk of transmission to a partner.

10. Most couples decide together how to reduce the risk.

[Italics, bold font and underlines mine]
[End of ASHA information.]
[The following is from Quest Diagnostics' ® website]
(www.questdiagnostics.com)

A herpes infection..."hides" in a certain type of nerve cell, causing recurrent outbreaks of sores in some people. Recurring infections can be triggered by factors such as stress, fatigue, sunlight, or another infection, such as a cold or flu. Medication can relieve symptoms and shorten the duration of the outbreaks, but medication cannot cure the infection.

- **Polymerase chain reaction (PCR) test.** PCR testing can be done on cells or fluid from a sore or on blood or on other fluid

Chapter 13: Sex Sobriety

(such as spinal fluid). PCR detects the genetic material (DNA) of the HSV virus. This test can distinguish between HSV-1 and HSV-2. The PCR test is not commonly done on skin lesions, but it is best for testing spinal fluid, for rare cases in which herpes may be causing infection in or around the brain.

[End of Quest Diagnostics' ® information.]

There are other tests that are more commonly used than the PCR test, such as a blood test or a culture from an outbreak. (Cultures have been said to have a high inaccuracy rate, producing false negatives. The virus often dies in transition to the lab.) When testing for STDs, you have to specifically request a herpes test be included or else they generally won't test for it. (This may differ in some regions.) There are different kinds of herpes blood tests that you should be familiar with. One kind (HSV 1&2 IgG) shows if you've ever been exposed to it and distinguishes between type 1 and type 2, and others such as HSV 1&2 IgM only shows if it is a recent infection or in an active state at the time of testing, and does not distinguish between HSV-1 and HSV-2.

According to HerpeSelect (www.herpeselect.com), the two manufacturers that offer FDA approved testing are HerpeSelect by Focus Diagnostics and Trinity Biotech. There is a test from another source that is said to be very accurate. The test is called Herpes Western Blot, and it is from the University of Washington. Be sure to speak to your healthcare professional to get the proper test.

As stated earlier, condoms are not completely effective and there are areas that they don't reach and cannot protect. I've read testimonies where people acquired herpes and they used a condom when it happened. Aside from the condom being ineffective in some areas and scenarios, viruses can be transmitted by practices such as touching someone's genital area and then touching yourself, being in the sheets or using the same towel that contain someone else's bodily fluids, and other methods of genital or fluid contact that may not even involve intercourse.

[The following is from the CDC.]

HIV / AIDS:
What is HIV?

HIV (human immunodeficiency virus) is the virus that causes AIDS. This virus may be passed from one person to another when infected blood, semen, or vaginal secretions come in contact with an uninfected person's broken skin or mucous membranes*. In addition, infected pregnant women can pass HIV to their baby during pregnancy or delivery, as well as through breast-feeding. People with HIV have what is called HIV infection. Some of these people will develop AIDS as a result of their HIV infection.

   11. A mucous membrane is wet, thin tissue found in certain openings to the human body. These can include the mouth, eyes, nose, vagina, rectum, and opening of the penis.

Chapter 13: Sex Sobriety

What is AIDS?

AIDS stands for **A**cquired **I**mmuno**d**eficiency **S**yndrome.

Acquired – means that the disease is not hereditary but develops after birth from contact with a disease causing agent (in this case, HIV).

Immunodeficiency – means that the disease is characterized by a weakening of the immune system.

Syndrome – refers to a group of symptoms that collectively indicate or characterize a disease. In the case of AIDS this can include the development of certain infections and/or cancers, as well as a decrease in the number of certain cells in a person's immune system.

A diagnosis of AIDS is made by a physician using specific clinical or laboratory standards.

How does HIV cause AIDS?

HIV destroys a certain kind of blood cell (CD4+ T cells) which is crucial to the normal function of the human immune system. In fact, loss of these cells in people with HIV is an extremely powerful predictor of the development of AIDS. Studies of thousands of people have revealed that most people infected with HIV carry the virus for years before enough damage is done to the immune system for AIDS to develop. However, sensitive tests have shown a strong connection between the amount of HIV in the blood and the decline in CD4+ T cells and the development of AIDS. Reducing the amount of virus in the body with anti-retroviral therapies can dramatically slow the destruction of a person's immune system.

Why do some people make statements that HIV does not cause AIDS?

The epidemic of HIV and AIDS has attracted much attention both within and outside the medical and scientific communities. Much of this attention comes from the many social issues related to this disease such as sexuality, drug use, and poverty. Although the scientific evidence is overwhelming and compelling that HIV is the cause of AIDS, the disease process is still not completely understood. This incomplete understanding has led some persons to make statements that AIDS is not caused by an infectious agent or is caused by a virus that is not HIV. This is not only misleading, but may have dangerous consequences. Before the discovery of HIV, evidence from epidemiologic studies involving tracing of patients' sex partners and cases occurring in persons receiving transfusions of blood or blood clotting products had clearly indicated that the underlying cause of the condition was an infectious agent. Infection with HIV has been the sole common factor shared by AIDS cases throughout the world among men who have sex with men, transfusion recipients, persons with hemophilia, sex partners of infected persons, children born to infected women, and occupationally exposed health care workers.

The conclusion after more than 20 years of scientific research is that people, if exposed to HIV through sexual contact or injecting drug use for example, may become

Chapter 13: Sex Sobriety

infected with HIV. If they become infected, most will eventually develop AIDS.

[NOTE FROM THE AUTHOR:]

While some debate about the cause and origin of AIDS, the important thing is to know your status and to make good decisions to avoid infection. For the alarming statistics of HIV / AIDS in the African American community and other details on the subject, go to www.cdc.gov.

[End Note]

Can I get HIV from kissing?

On the Cheek:

HIV is not transmitted casually, so kissing on the cheek is very safe. Even if the other person has the virus, your unbroken skin is a good barrier. No one has become infected from such ordinary social contact as dry kisses, hugs, and handshakes.

Open-Mouth Kissing:

Open-mouth kissing is considered a very low-risk activity for the transmission of HIV. However, prolonged open-mouth kissing could damage the mouth or lips and allow HIV to pass from an infected person to a partner and then enter the body through cuts or sores in the mouth.

Because of this possible risk, the CDC recommends against open-mouth kissing with an infected partner.

One case suggests that a woman became infected with HIV from her sex partner through exposure to contaminated blood during open-mouth kissing.

Can I get HIV from oral sex?

Yes, it is possible for either partner to become infected with HIV through performing or receiving oral sex. There have been a few cases of HIV transmission from performing oral sex on a person infected with HIV. While no one knows exactly what the degree of risk is, evidence suggests that the risk is less than that of unprotected anal or vaginal sex.

If the person performing oral sex has HIV, blood from their mouth may enter the body of the person receiving oral sex through

- the lining of the urethra (the opening at the tip of the penis);
- the lining of the vagina or cervix;
- the lining of the anus; or
- directly into the body through small cuts or open sores.

If the person receiving oral sex has HIV, their blood, semen (cum), pre-seminal fluid (pre-cum), or vaginal fluid may contain the virus. Cells lining the mouth of the

Chapter 13: Sex Sobriety

person performing oral sex may allow HIV to enter their body.

The risk of HIV transmission increases

- if the person performing oral sex has cuts or sores around or in their mouth or throat;
- if the person receiving oral sex ejaculates in the mouth of the person performing oral sex; or
- if the person receiving oral sex has another sexually transmitted disease (STD).

Not having (abstaining from) sex is the most effective way to avoid HIV.

If you choose to perform oral sex, and your partner is male,

- use a latex condom on the penis; or
- if you or your partner is allergic to latex, plastic (polyurethane) condoms can be used.

Studies have shown that latex condoms are very effective, though not perfect, in preventing HIV transmission when used correctly and consistently. If either partner is allergic to latex, plastic (polyurethane) condoms for either the male or female can be used. For more information about latex condoms, see "Male Latex Condoms and Sexually Transmitted Diseases."

If you choose to have oral sex, and your partner is female,

- use a latex barrier (such as a natural rubber latex sheet, a dental dam or a cut-open condom that makes a square) between your mouth and the vagina. A latex barrier such as a dental dam reduces the risk of blood or vaginal fluids entering your mouth. Plastic food wrap also can be used as a barrier.

If you choose to share sex toys with your partner, such as dildos or vibrators,

- each partner should use a new condom on the sex toy; and
- be sure to clean sex toys between each use.

Are "lesbians" or other women who have sex with women at risk for HIV?

Female-to-female transmission of HIV appears to be a rare occurrence. However, there are case reports of female-to-female transmission of HIV. The well documented risk of female-to-male transmission of HIV shows that vaginal secretions and menstrual blood may contain the virus and that mucous membrane (e.g., oral, vaginal) exposure to these secretions has the potential to lead to HIV infection.

Chapter 13: Sex Sobriety

In order to reduce the risk of HIV transmission, women who have sex with women should do the following:

- Avoid exposure of a mucous membrane, such as the mouth, (especially non-intact tissue) to vaginal secretions and menstrual blood.
- Use condoms consistently and correctly each and every time for sexual contact with men or when using sex toys. Sex toys should not be shared. No barrier methods for use during oral sex have been evaluated as effective by the FDA. However, natural rubber latex sheets, dental dams, cut open condoms, or plastic wrap may offer some protection from contact with body fluids during oral sex and possibly reduce the risk of HIV transmission.
- Know your own and your partner's HIV status. This knowledge can help uninfected women begin and maintain behavioral changes that reduce the risk of becoming infected. For women who are found to be infected, it can assist in getting early treatment and avoiding infecting others.

How well does HIV survive outside the body?

Scientists and medical authorities agree that HIV does not survive well outside the body, making the possibility of environmental transmission remote. HIV is found in varying concentrations or amounts in blood, semen, vaginal fluid, breast milk, saliva, and tears. To obtain data on the survival of HIV, laboratory studies have required the use of artificially high concentrations of laboratory-grown virus. Although these unnatural concentrations of HIV can be kept alive for days or even weeks under precisely controlled and limited laboratory conditions, CDC studies have shown that drying of even these high concentrations of HIV reduces the amount of infectious virus by 90 to 99 percent within several hours. Since the HIV concentrations used in laboratory studies are much higher than those actually found in blood or other specimens, drying of HIV-infected human blood or other body fluids reduces the theoretical risk of environmental transmission to that which has been observed – essentially zero. Incorrect interpretations of conclusions drawn from laboratory studies have in some instances caused unnecessary alarm.

Results from laboratory studies should not be used to assess specific personal risk of infection because (1) the amount of virus studied is not found in human specimens or elsewhere in nature, and (2) no one has been identified as infected with HIV due to contact with an environmental surface. Additionally, HIV is unable to reproduce outside its living host (unlike many bacteria or fungi, which may do so under suitable conditions), except under laboratory conditions; therefore, it does not spread or maintain infectiousness outside its host.

How long after a possible exposure should I wait to get tested for HIV?
The tests commonly used to detect HIV infection are actually looking for antibodies produced by an individual's immune system when they are exposed to HIV. Most people will develop detectable antibodies within two to

Chapter 13: Sex Sobriety

eight weeks (the average is 25 days). Ninety seven percent will develop antibodies in the first three months following the time of their infection. In very rare cases, it can take up to six months to develop antibodies to HIV.

Where can I get information about treatments?

CDC recommends that you be in the care of a licensed health care provider, preferably one with experience treating people living with HIV. Your health care provider can assist you with treatment information and guidance.

Detailed information on specific treatments is available from the Department of Health and Human Services' AIDSinfo ◀ . Information on enrolling in clinical trials is also available at AIDSinfo ◀ . You may contact AIDSinfo by phone at 1-800-448-0440 (English and Spanish) or 1-888-480-3739 (TTY).

Not having (abstaining from) sex is the most effective way to avoid transmitting HIV to others. If you choose to have sex, use a latex condom to help protect your partner from HIV and other STDs. Studies have shown that latex condoms are very effective, though not perfect, in preventing HIV transmission when used correctly and consistently. If either partner is allergic to latex, plastic (polyurethane) condoms for either the male or female can be used.

If you would like more information or have personal concerns, contact:

CDC-INFO:
1-800-CDC-INFO (232-4636)
TTY: 1-888-232-6348
In English, en Español
24 Hours/Day

Chancroid:

This is one of the STDs that I had never heard of. It's most common in developing nations, and there it can be epidemic. It is a genital ulcer disease that can be quite painful. It is spread by direct contact with the skin, and after 2 to 10 days, a pustule erupts that leaves a painful ulcer. There may be multiple ulcers that may be quite deep. In cases where the ulceration is extensive, scaring may be permanent even with medical treatment.

This is found more commonly in men. It has been reported that this is likely due to the connection of this disease and prostitution.

Treatment is usually successful, if the person's immune system is normal.

Safety!

The surest way to avoid transmission of sexually transmitted diseases, including genital herpes, is to abstain from sexual contact, or to be in a long-term mutually monogamous relationship with a partner who has been tested and is known to be uninfected.

Chapter 13: Sex Sobriety

[This marks the end of the information gathered from the CDC website–the following is a statement from the American Social Health Association.]

People who choose to be sexually active must have access to information and options to reduce their risk.
And for the millions of people who have previously acquired a viral sexually transmitted infection, effective measures must be taken to protect any future partners from infection.

[This marks the end of the ASHA information.]

Regarding the above STD information, there are serious decisions to be made. Know your status, and the status of your partner.

No One Excluded

We've got to do much better, especially in the Black community. We make up about 13% of the nation's population, yet it's now said that about 80% of all HIV cases currently being reported are of Black women; according to a most recent report. Many men (including HIV+ men) have multiple partners and have not taken heed to HIV warnings as other communities have. New HIV rates in the White community have declined greatly over the last few years. Young people are also being severely affected. I know of a high school where a blood drive was done. The blood drive coordinators came back to the school shortly afterwards and announced that

207

about half of the junior and senior class was HIV positive. It has been reported that another high school in the same metropolitan area is about 38% HIV positive. Parents, you may want to get your minor children tested.

Rolling The Dice

Most of us can't say we've always done everything to minimize the risks of STD's. I originally expected to go into more detail about safer methods, but if you knew for sure your partner had an STD, would you rely on a method and / or a condom? Some have chosen to do so, and some even choose not to use a condom with an STD+ person they're in a relationship with. For those who do make that decision, they do so with the knowledge of the situation, and that is their right and their choice to make. However, if you use a condom and your partner is positive, if the condom breaks or slips off, it leaves you in a vulnerable situation. (Go to www.ashastd.org and read the condom use do's and don'ts section.)

Some people speak of the fact that they get tested regularly, as if that's keeping them safe. If they don't know their partner's status, diagnosing a problem (while important) is far inferior to preventing it.

Chapter 13: Sex Sobriety

My Doctors' Advice

After breaking up from over ten years of marriage and then dating again, whenever I got a physical and / or an STD test, I had questions for my doctor. I knew about the importance of using a condom, but I wanted to know how to identify a partner with an STD *before* having sex at all. "What are the things to look for?" I asked eagerly. One doctor said, "It's really hard to do an STD examination on a date," with amusement in his facial expression. His suggestion? He said, "Bring her by with you and I'll do a thorough examination for you both." Another doctor echoed his advice. He said, "The best thing to do is for both of you to get tested and stay monogamous." Admittedly, that was not quite what I had in mind at the time. The reoccurring caution eventually changed my thinking. That, along with my research was the largest motivating factor in writing this part of the book.

What Can Be Done?

Even if someone practices cautious methods such as using a condom and not touching their partner's genital area during foreplay and then touching themselves, the only REAL way to be safe is to abstain—which many of us don't want to do. The next best thing: Get tested with a monogamous partner. Wait no less than 90 days and get tested again with neither of you having had sex in the mean time. Or, according to the information discussed earlier, waiting six months for the second test would detect 97% of sexually transmitted HIV infections, yet this requires both to be willing to do this, and the trust that both of you have remained abstinent during the incubation period between tests. Admittedly, this is a very challenging proposition. Especially for a recently sexually active person, to wait three to six months or more to have sex with a new partner is much easier said than done. If you have sex during this period, don't forget it's important to use a condom (or two) until the incubation risk is gone and you both tested negative again, if you choose to stop wearing them even then. The question is, how long does the incubation period last? I don't know if that has been confirmed in an absolute way, but I have heard to be complete in HIV testing you must test for seven years (that time *may* be shorter now with newer technology—consult your health professional). Any time frames you choose is your choice to make, but don't be in a rush to have unprotected sex. While I wanted to make STD information available to some who wouldn't have learned of it elsewhere, I understand human nature. The power of sexual attraction can occupy your inner "commander's seat" if you're not careful. With a little convenience of opportunity it's not hard to compromise. It was not an immediate undertaking for me to take a stand even after learning some of the things I did. During my writing (a span of several years), I've wrestled with compromise. Even now, I know that holding up under future challenges requires constant focus, but my resolve has become firm. If you're open to or looking for an intimate partner relationship, keep your mind on progressive, positive things. Stay busy—it helps. Prepare yourself; and I believe that when you're really ready for something, it must come.

Observe your partner's habits. For example, does

Chapter 13: Sex Sobriety

he or she want to have sex with you without a condom? If they do, don't flatter yourself and think it's because you're so wonderful. They probably have unprotected sex anytime their partner is willing.

A Different Kind of Socialite

We've heard of introverts and extroverts. A different kind of socialite is one I call a "sextrovert." They may be "Swingers" or people who participate in sex clubs, but not all sextroverts are that "out there." Some of them want to leave a sexual legacy for their own ego, and some of them just have casual sex freely because that's one of their forms of recreation. Often, they will admit that they don't want to know, talk, or think about the dangers of their lifestyle. One thing is true, however: The bliss of ignorance can only last for so long. Then again, some of them are sextroverts because they know their status is positive and they're fearless because they feel they have nothing to lose.

Have you ever been involved with a sextrovert? I've had one tell me (like the Marines) she's "just looking for a few good men!" Please understand, I'm not criticizing people who choose this lifestyle, just sending a word of caution. Also, if you are seeking a D.T.A. or D.T.R., steer clear of sextroverts. They think that "monogamy" is some type of fancy furniture.

****

Again, don't let fear of a positive result prevent you from getting tested. If your status is negative (showing no disease), then it's good to know and can add to your peace of mind. Stay conscious of how to preserve your status. If it is positive, then with advice from a healthcare professional you'll have vital knowledge on how to go forward. You'll know how to get treatment and the changes you may need to make in your routine, sexually and otherwise. Whether you're in a relationship or not, everyone should know their own status. If you know your status is clear, it typically makes a person more inclined to need to know their partner (or prospective partner) is STD free also. Still, use common sense. Don't let someone's words alone be your deciding factor!

0% Risk?

A friend said, "You can get tested together and your partner could cheat and you could still get something." Of course, that could happen to anyone, even in marriage. There are never guarantees; unless you never have sex, never kiss, never have a work or other incident that exposes you to someone's blood or fluids, never try on clothes someone else has tried on, never use anyone's linen, and never eat or drink behind anyone. While this sounds very thorough, I'm sure there's something I left out. The point is you do what you can, and what makes sense.

How Did This Happen?

The data above says about one in four people age 12 and up have HSV-2, and 50 to 80% have HSV-1. A lab testing employee I interviewed told me that

Chapter 13: Sex Sobriety

HSV-1 is now thought to be about 85%. If this is only one infection, and you add to that HPV (the virus that causes genital warts), and this does not even address the more than 1,039,000 in this country that has HIV, or HSV-2 or the curable infections, what does this mean for our children and grandchildren? Will anyone ask why the "powers that be" have been so silent instead of making sure the public was alerted before these rates got so out of control? We've heard about HIV / AIDS, but that's not all we need to know about. Many will say, "The information is there, but people will do what they want to do." While I do agree, it's just like a caution sign for hazardous road conditions. We could just see it when we get there, but how much better to be advised at repeated intervals when society is being severely affected! If we did have these warnings more pronounced consistently through time (not just once or a few times) and changed our behavior, then how would that have affected the medical / pharmaceutical, health / life insurance, and entertainment industries, just to name a few? Now that we are aware, let's stay awake.

Life After Positive Status?

What of those that know they're STD / STI positive, with no known cure? There are some really good people out there, who may have either not been careful enough or their significant other may have been unfaithful and given them a positive status (not to mention the non sexual means of transmission). With all of the caution I speak of herein, it is in no way intended to ostracize anyone. The previous information shows that a positive status could happen (or even if it didn't—*could have* happened) to almost anyone.

For those who are STD+ / STI+, single and are dating, it is very embarrassing and uncomfortable to discuss their status as they get to know someone. Not only do you not want to air your business to someone unworthy, but you don't know that they'll keep your confidential matters confidential.

I mentioned earlier in the chapter "The Vibe" about the need for dialog on relationship issues. How the STD+ / STI+ can date with honesty and dignity is one topic that can be expounded upon more. There are community support groups where people have a positive status for HIV, herpes or others and they can correspond online or even at meetings in the community. There are even websites devoted to this. People sometimes date within these groups, yet some people may prefer not to connect with others in this way. They may be uncomfortable with the idea, and / or prefer to meet someone and date the traditional way. My only advice on that is: First of all, if you chose not to discuss your status at this time, ***don't have sex*** with the person. If they discuss it or hint towards sex, tell them you're not ready for sex at this time, that you want to take it slower. If it comes to the test process and the other person knows (or says) their status is negative and they speak of only pursuing a negative partner, you could just drop off the scene (or fade out) if you're still not ready to discuss it. They can assume you just didn't click, or whatever they'd like to assume.

Secondly, many are living very functional lives and feeling good, not sickly, while they carry on with life. Again, it shows how normal their life can be because many don't even know they're positive. The point here is

Chapter 13: Sex Sobriety

that many are not only happy and productive but some have found love with a non-positive partner who knows their status. It's important to know that having a positive status even with HIV, doesn't have to mean life is now over. Medicines have improved life much better than it did twenty years ago. *Just be honest with your partner before having sex with them.* It would also be fair to them if you tell them before their feelings got very deep.

Some herbalists have made claims that they have cured diseases that are said to have no cure. Whether that is true or not I cannot say, but I will say that I do believe that on this divinely created planet, natural remedies can do some remarkable things. I believe it is incumbent upon each person to seek any information that may lead them to legitimate and healthy options, while keeping in mind that there are some unscrupulous people who'll sell you the sky if you let them.

Those who have a positive status should know that if they are careless, they not only jeopardize others but could still worsen their situation. I believe most aware positive status people would use a condom, but for those who don't, feeling they have nothing to lose, keep in mind that those with HIV are more susceptible to Herpes, or could acquire Hepatitis or full blown AIDS. Those with Herpes are more susceptible to HIV, and could also acquire Hepatitis or AIDS, just to name a few scenarios. For those who have an STD and seek to "share it" with others, imagine if someone did that to one of your loved ones. There's always karma and jail / prison time.

Plan B, C, & D
The Men Women Choose When They Don't Have What They *Really* Want!

STD / STI Review Summary — This is not a complete listing, but for more information visit the websites listed in the Appendix of this book.

Disease:	Description / Symptoms:
HIV / AIDS	**AIDS** stands for **A**cquired **I**mmuno**d**eficiency **S**yndrome. HIV/AIDS attacks the immune system, making a person more susceptible to various other illnesses. It is possible to become infected through oral sex, along with the more common means of transmission such as anal and vaginal sex. Approximately 38.6 million people world wide are infected with HIV/AIDS, and over one million people in the United States have the infection. There is no known medical cure for HIV/AIDS.
Herpes Type 1 (HSV-1)	Herpes type 1 is one of the most common sexually transmitted infections. Ironically, however, it can easily be spread without having sex at all, but simply by kissing someone while the virus is in an 'active' state. This is why children at times get the virus. HSV-1 causes what is commonly called "cold soars". HSV-1 can be spread even when there is no visible soar or blister. Active HSV-1 during oral sex can cause genital herpes to the recipient. It is now estimated that up to 80-85% of all adults in America have HSV-1. There is no known medical cure for this infection.
Herpes Type 2 (HSV-2)	Herpes type 2 causes genital herpes. It is estimated that 20-25% of all Americans have genital herpes, and 80-90% of them don't know they have it. They may have had no or mild symptoms, where they may overlook the symptoms all together. Outbreaks often occur due to stress or anxiety, and those outbreaks (soars) can be very painful. HSV-2 can be transmitted while using a condom, and there is no known medical cure for HSV-2.
Genital Warts (HPV)	Genital warts are caused by human papillomavirus (HPV). HPV is said to be the most common sexually transmitted infection. In some cases, HPV can cause cancer in the cervix, uterus, vagina, penis, or anus. There is treatment available for the warts caused by the virus, but not for the virus itself. The body's immune system can sometimes overcome the virus on its own, most commonly after age 30 (but not in all cases). The infection can easily go undetected, and can be present without causing any symptoms at all. There is no known medical cure.

Chapter 14:

Better Choices

Chapter 14:
Better Choices

Everything we do, have, and experience is a matter of the decisions we make, with only a few exceptions. We have been groomed by T.V., movies, music, fashion, videos, and commercialism, and other fictional forms of entertainment. While entertainment is needed for a balance in life, many people are unable to decipher the difference between that entertainment and real life.

Let's Put The Puzzle Together

Some of the single person's challenges are: We have too much pride, and don't want to seem like we want a prospective partner more than they may want us. We are paralyzed by fear of rejection, and driven to insanity by fear of commitment and a partner's infidelity. We're sometimes immature around someone we want to be around, and mess up opportunities to make things last longer. We listen to people's negativity (and hate) and / or we disseminate it, without justification. Get the picture? *WE'VE GOT MUCH WORK TO DO!!!* We are slow to communicate, when we need to just speak our minds. If you want to be with someone more, then say so. If you don't feel your friendship or relationship is working out, then say so. Don't bury your feelings until things are terminal. We all have something to keep an eye or handle on, regarding our own issues in dating. Whatever our weaknesses are, we just have to keep working on them. Let's **stop playing games.** As outrageous as your thoughts may be, there's someone out there who will accept you and your thinking. Think of the serial killers and terrorists who get fan mail from women saying they would marry this person. That's an extreme example, but the point is; be yourself (unless you're a killer or terrorist). Even if you want multiple partners and can't commit, let the partner you're with know. There are more people who think like you than you know. If this partner won't have it, then you can find one that will.

Often people complain about what they do and don't have in relationships. In my opinion, unless they're trying to do something to change the situation in a productive way, they don't really need it to change. Let's get our relationships in order. Let's talk about what we need and want. Respect others, and just find your niche. Put aside the hurt from the past. Learn from it, and then move forward. Easier said than done, but it's something that many of us need to continually work on.

A Better Quality Life?

Regarding the STD information: This is not my data but rather public data that has been available for many years. (Don't hate the messenger!) Regarding the testing, it cancels out the "one night stand" setting. The point? I'm going to state my opinion of the best situation, but I know that each person must do what works for them. As adults, we must make decisions and be willing

Chapter 14: Better Choices

to accept any outcome based on those decisions. A person can be personally and financially successful being single, but in my opinion, generally it's easier to achieve a higher level of success (success is open to personal definition) when they're either married or in a committed relationship. *In a productive relationship,* they can then focus more effectively on their families, goals, hobbies, businesses, careers, etc. This is one of the reasons they become financially successful. Along with being driven by their determination to succeed, they haven't spread themselves too thin by the draw of energy from singleness. You can focus on where you want to go in life with fewer distractions. Those distractions may include talking for hours per week on the phone, sometimes with various different people. Dating does require time, but if you're honest with yourself, you sometimes know the people you're spending time with are not what you're looking for anyway. That's why the "no non-sense dating" is important. Don't be afraid to say who you are in fear of turning someone away. If they don't want the real you, you don't need them. Even without a relationship, you can date successfully, as I feel I have learned to do. In my opinion that simply involves knowing your needs and wants, being honest with yourself and others, doing all that is in your control to have a safe and pleasant experience, and avoiding drama. Dating successfully doesn't have to mean that you're in a relationship, or that you have a date every weekend.

Some people are not inclined to marriage or commitment and would make a poor commitment partner. Know yourself enough to know if this would be you, and if so don't do it. Don't get involved with someone you don't really want just for the sake of having or marrying someone. Yet, if more people had a committed relationship in mind rather than having as many options as they can, in my opinion it would make for more stability and success, even if they didn't choose to get married. Don't get me wrong, some people are single and happy with that and are doing well, so again, do what works for you. Many ladies may say, "But the men out there aren't ready for a relationship, so my choices are slim," and many men would say the same about you ladies. If both of us get our priorities in order, it'll be more options for both sexes. Don't forget the gatherings with the 4 Level Dialog as discussed in "The Vibe", and also consider other options.

Singles' Groups and Websites—Consider It

Considering the number of options out there and the challenge of meeting, I'm in favor of singles groups and matchmaking companies or websites. It doesn't mean you're desperate. For those who don't want to seek a potential life partner in a night club (understandably so), it's a way to meet someone who you know is looking for someone, isn't into immature games (hopefully) and can somewhat cut to the chase. For most of us, I think having a consistent partner is the goal to have. Once you find someone who will be that S.O. to you, then give it your best shot. Work to make it successful and be faithful to it. Many of us carry blame for unsuccessful relationships of the past. Let's move forward and work to make the future a solid one. If it doesn't work out down the road, the way you handle it can at least make it good while it lasts. Stay true to it and

Chapter 14: Better Choices

perhaps the next relationship will be successful.

Heavy Decisions

Some who are currently in a relationship they're not happy with may feel the grass is greener on the other side. If there are no major issues (especially if you're in deep or married) then maybe the information in this book can help you (or give you motivation) to work it out. I'm not suggesting that someone in a bad situation should stay. It's your decision, just be sure to make an informed one. Many men in Atlanta, Ga. hear the same info I've heard for years; "There's 10 or 14 women to every man." While there is a large gay / bisexual community that has a bearing on heterosexual options, I think based on my census research, that ratio may be exaggerated. I think a possibly exaggerated ratio, along with other factors has a bearing on men's thinking, as if they're kids on a playground. Men, just like women, you don't have as many good options as you may think. If you have or find a good woman, hold on to her! The same applies to women; if you have a good man, hold on to him! Don't let things get stale.

Some decide, based on the number of options they have, to get involved with someone who's in a relationship or already married. You deserve better for yourself. You deserve a relationship with commitment to you only. Also keep in mind that you will want your spouse to be faithful to you when you're in a relationship, so send out good so that good can return to you.

Some may seek out groups to get STD testing together in order to have multiple sex partner options. For those who choose these things, keep in mind that the door for repercussions and drama is wide open. No one can dictate to another adult on these things. Yet in my opinion, it is not a course that produces wellness, happiness and peace, but rather stress and regret. The scenario of testing in a group is better than not testing at all, but just be willing to accept any consequences that come from your decisions.

Who Am I?

Who is Nkansa Landis Casterlow? I'd say I'm an idealist in many ways, who has observed people and the dating scene and sought to make sense of it all for myself, in relation to life. Like many of us, I've felt regret over the plight of relationships (and learned from my own) and would love to see the success rate of relationships increase greatly. I feel a large part of that is making sure we're ready ourselves, and considering our *chase, our vibe, and our needs and wants* when we're considering a relationship. For those of us who are still in the selection process, we can get ourselves off to a good start by choosing the right partner.

While I'm sure it's clear how I feel about Sue and her priorities, I understand *anyone* pursuing financial success. Those who have the Sue mentality just limit themselves quite a bit. As of this writing, I have much to learn about wealth. However, it is my goal that as I learn and grow financially, to teach others what I learn so that they can likewise improve themselves. This is not simply to show someone how to become Plan A for someone who would not have appreciated them before, but because the need for it is great. Remember ladies; if you get a man with good character, the rest can come!

Chapter 14: Better Choices

Because of my views on sex in dating, I'm not, as some may think, asexual in my views or interest. Far from it! I believe sex is (or can be) one of life's greatest pleasures, particularly in the right situation. I have even written poetry and song lyrics that express appreciation for sexuality. I just want the best quality of life possible, realized by good decisions. I'm a single (divorced) father of one child, who looks forward to sharing a life journey with a woman who is my complement; in its due time.

I hope you have found this reading informative, resourceful, and mentally stimulating. Much peace, success, good health and prosperity to you!

Critic's Corner

My critics may say:

"I've heard that you've admitted to being guilty of infidelity in the past; therefore, your words have less merit."
I do believe in the things that build a strong relationship, trust and fidelity being a large part of that. I've made mistakes and bad decisions, learned much, and want to share things with others that may be of help to them.

"Your advice on abstaining from sex for so long is not practical."
As I have stated, I am fully aware that it's easier said than done. I believe that if we make ourselves more ready for commitment and fusing our lives with another person (mentally, psychologically, spiritually and financially—yes, I said financially) then we'll be more prepared to enjoy the

good things while being responsible. Like doctors and their craft of medicine, life is a lifelong practice. Let's work on it as long as we have it!

"Your book speaks as if all women are the same—chasing money. I'm not like that, and I don't even know any women like that."
Yes, believe it or not, I've heard this. I just can't believe that. I think unless you or your associates (or both) have been living in a cave, you know someone like Sue! I know all women aren't like this, and as I said from the outset, if the shoe doesn't fit, guess what? It's not your shoe.

"How can you talk about sex and quote scriptures in the same book?"
While I do feel that acceptance of scriptural principles are very useful in life, this book is not intended to be a religious guide, and I don't profess to be a good spiritual example. However, I write not only from the perspectives I've come to acquire, but also from a part of my foundation. My objective herein is to give useful information. There is information about sex herein that can be beneficial to married couples also, so each person will have to tailor the information to their life.

"Some of the things you talk about are so personal. Your personal matters shouldn't be discussed so openly in a book."
Some of my family may argue this one! Though my life is far from perfection, I feel I would lose some of the value in my message if I tried to detach myself from it. I write because I have something to say, and revealing faults or

Chapter 14: Better Choices

something personal in this case is a choice I have made.

"The information you give is depressing!"
There are some things herein that I would agree can sound disheartening, but my objective is to help people see things in a different way. Not in a dismal way, but a way that reassesses practical priorities. Once we do that based on realistic thinking, then we can benefit. Bitter or sweet; truth IS. Truth doesn't bend to suit us; we must bend to benefit from it.

"I've done / I know the numbers and your screening chart statistics are wrong!"
Congratulations on your research or knowledge of important data! As I mentioned in the paragraph before the stats, this is not a science book and the numbers are in no way exact. I did, however, seek to be reasonably close, all limitations as they are. Even where I may be off in areas and the options are actually higher than I have indicated, when you consider the ideas in the section "Challenging Truths—Fewer Options", the point remains that we may not have as many ideal options as we may think. Along with our very specific expectations and requirements, these things profoundly affect the bigger picture.

APPENDIX

Each website is fully responsible for its own content. Nkansa L. Casterlow is not responsible for errors or any activity associated with them. The following sites may be helpful for:

Health info:

www.cdc.gov

www.ashastd.org

www.questdiagnostics.com ®

www.herpeselect.com

Mental health:

http://www.cdc.gov/nchs/fastats/druguse.htm

http://www.mhsource.com/resource/mh.html

Population stats:

www.census.gov

www.epodunk.com

Domestic violence victim info/resources:

www.ndvh.org

Height info:

www.tallpages.com/uk/index.php?pag=ukstatist.php

Other sites that may be helpful:

www.blackhealthcare.com

www.nblca.org

www.stdweb.com

www.herpes-coldsores.com